MISSING
A True Story Of A Childhood LOST

Marnie Grundman

ISBN 978-0-995192003

Printed by Meraki House Publishing
Cover Photo: Cheshire Academy middle school class photo taken a
few months prior to Marnie going MISSING.

DEDICATION

To my father who unintentionally gave me the courage to write this book through his validation and unconditional love. I miss you every day. Thank you for making me whole.

To my children who taught me how to love and gave me the gift of self-forgiveness. I love you all to the moon, beyond and back.

To Donna B., You and your family fed my heart and gifted me with the ability to bond. I love you with all of my heart.

- Your little sweetheart

CONTENTS

FORWARD

The book you are holding in your hands, the story your fingers have begun to unravel before you is the story of my mother. Like you, each page I lifted was the first time I was exposed to this beautiful woman's tragic struggle to survive; this little girl's disrupted coming of age. Yet, it's this book that is both an end and a beginning of a journey. The end of my mother's running, yet the beginning of something far scarier; looking back. The end of her suffering but the beginning of her healing. The end of our family's denial and the beginning of our reconciliation. The end of our, the readers naivety and the digestion of Adam and Eve's apple of truth. The end of all our son's and daughter's running away and the beginning of their journeys home, maybe not to an address but definitely to a heart, to love.

I understood at a young age that I was going to be the man of my mother's life and I have been the most consistent man in her life, 29 years and counting. I always knew bits and pieces of the causes of her running. But before I opened this book, like you, I never knew where she ran to. As an athletic runner myself, I know the freedom each step away gives to a powerless child. As a young adult I know the vulnerable liberation it feels to face the horrors which cause us to run. The best embrace I can give my mother, and to you who will inevitably absorb or trigger long forgotten pain, comes from the words of a beautiful poet *"our hearts break as many times as it takes for it to open."* - Rumi

My mother didn't write this book for sympathy, or vengeance, she wrote this book for love. She wrote her story so that when we open this book, we may open our hearts in the process. That we may open our hearts and our doors to all the abandoned children like her, like ourselves.

This is not a book, but a cry from the child inside you, to open your heart to yourself.

- James A. Hernandez

I held my babies almost nonstop until they were almost a year and a half old. At 7 and 9 years old I still sing songs to them before bed and I cannot fathom the idea of anything less than a face full of kisses and two rounds of hugs before I tuck them in and turn out the lights. They're my children, I know no other way of existing than to love them wholeheartedly, than to express that love with all of my being.

I learned this in large part from my mother. Growing up, I never once - not for a day in my life - doubted that my mother loved me. And yet, it is a miracle that she even knew how.

I read her story as more than just her daughter; I read it as a woman who was once a child, a teenager, a young adult, and then a mother herself. A child who went to ballet lessons and had great big birthday parties with delicious home-made theme cakes; a child who went trick-or-treating in ornate, handmade Halloween costumes, and who loved when her mom came with her on school field trips. A teenager who was happy when her mom chaperoned her senior homecoming dance and saw her crowned queen, and who had her pick of the best colleges after graduating high school with honours. A young adult who went off to the University of Miami on scholarship, who had normal dates with nice boys, enjoying the innocence of holding hands and first kisses by the beautiful Miami Oceanside. The very place where her mom used to take her swimming as a little girl; the very place where her mom went missing as a little girl.

Her childhood was stolen from her, first at the hands of the people who were supposed to love her most, take care of her, protect her, and then by the monsters that go bump in the night, the ones most of us never have to know about firsthand.

She never even had a chance.
And yet... she survived. More than that, she *surthrived*.

Join my mother as she takes you on a journey from missing to healing, from struggle to empowerment, as she rises up against all odds to become... Whole. Fearless. Happy.

My mother, above all else, is a shining light. For me, her daughter. For you, reading this book, with your own history and demons to heal from. She is courage, fortitude, and grace. She is living proof that no matter what life hands you, you have within you the spirit to rise, to rewrite the outcome of your story, to create a life of love, of happiness.

I am proud to introduce you to Marnie Grundman, my mother, who was once a missing child.

-Jade Alexandra

PREFACE

On June 20th, 1980 at the age of thirteen, I became a missing child. In the blink of an eye I went from living in an upper middle class home with a soft bed and all the food I could eat, to being a child of the streets.

No more middle school. No possibility of high school. There would never be a homecoming dance. No big prom date. No cap and gown fitting for graduation. No walking down the halls with my schoolmates giggling while gripping a love note from my boyfriend. No homework or big exams to cram for. No field trips. No family vacations. No birthday celebrations. No trying out for the cheerleading squad or basketball team. No ordinary rites of passage. It was all gone, lost forever.

This is my story of survival and eventual *surthrival*.

INTRODUCTION

I have lived the majority of my life in the dark, ashamed of my time on the streets. Embarrassed that I had my first child at seventeen. Ashamed that I didn't complete my education. Damaged because of the sexual abuse I suffered at the hands of both strangers and a relative. I have realized that to fully heal I have to let the light shine in. I have to take proud ownership of the life I have been ashamed of and felt damaged by for so long.

This book is not so much about what led me to the streets, as it is about my life on the streets. I will have to share some of the reasons why, but I am not interested taking in vengeance on my perpetrators. This is about me, my journey, and my healing not them. For years after I was a runaway I looked for books that focused on people like me. I wanted something I could relate to, something that would help me to feel that I am not alone. I still have yet to find that book, so I am sharing my truth in the hopes that my words will help others.

I am going to focus on the three plus years living the life of the girl/woman I invented to survive life on the streets. The invention of that person was so powerful that I almost forgot my real identity and where I came from. I responded to my made up name better than I would have responded to my given name. For 3 years "Marnie" was just a girl I used to know. Someone worthless and better forgotten. In many ways that is how it all came to pass. I knew, I believed, that I was better forgotten. I knew I would be easily forgotten.

1 NEVER JUDGE A BOOK BY ITS COVER

You never really know where a person came from unless they share their past with you. I have, for most of my life, been a person who only shares what is necessary… to the extreme; until now, that is. I have kept my past a secret as I was enveloped by shame and fear of discovery. When you look at me you would never guess that I was a runaway, a missing child, or that ever I lived on the streets. Beginning at the age of thirteen I lived a hungry, dirty and destitute existence; an existence that my current outer shell would never give away. From the outside, the only thing a passer-by sees is an attractive, well put-together, middle-aged woman. No one would ever be able to tell that I came from years of mental abuse, physical/sexual abuse and neglect at the hands of my mother and other family members. It was that abuse and neglect that forced me to end up on streets.

If you spoke with me you would most likely conclude that I am college educated. The people that know me well - and even those that do not know me particularly well - would never guess or believe where I actually came from, or what my truth is. My standard response when people ask about my background is the following: I was born in Montreal, moved to Miami and then lived in New York while attending boarding school in Connecticut. I leave out the runaway/missing child part. I leave out the fact that I left school in grade eight. If there are any questions, it's about university and I have that covered as well. I quit two semesters shy of my nursing degree to pursue art. While all of the above is true it doesn't begin to scratch the surface of my history.

The truth is that I have literally lived many lives… Many lifetimes. I have recreated myself over and over again. I was forced to live a lie and take on a new identity. I was forced to change my age, name and familial history to avoid discovery. For three years right smack in the middle of my adolescence, I lived the life of a completely invented person. A person that I will introduce to you as my story unfolds. While most teenagers are simply trying to figure out who they are and where they fit in, I was lost in someone that didn't even really exist. With this book, I will for the first time in my life be living as me, as all of *me*, the real me.

I was born into an upper middle class home; the type of home where people do not want to believe that bad things happen. Abuse and alcoholism in the sixties and seventies was largely associated with people from impoverished homes, the lower class. We now know that child abuse and neglect have no socio-economic boundaries. But, even with this not so new-found knowledge, we still rush to judgment. It is human nature. Even if the presence of abuse is believed, the acknowledgment of it is often diminished. The thought is that if you lived a comfortable lifestyle the abuse couldn't be that bad. I wrote an article that was posted on a popular website not too long ago about the abuse that I suffered at the hands of my mother. I cannot begin to tell you how many people posted things like "I had the same kind of mother but we were poor, must have been nice to live in a big house and go to boarding school." This type of sentiment is a big part of the reason I am sharing my story.

We need to break through this barrier, this stigma. We need to realize – to validate - that abuse doesn't feel better because of a materially better environment. Pain is not measured by what we do or don't have. We need to continue to speak out, to set the victims free. We need to stop adding to their pain by punishing them for coming from a more comfortable background. We also need to stop protecting the abusers who hide behind their posh doors. These abusers are master manipulators who know how to use their class as protection. They are keenly aware that people will be slower to believe that a child from the upper side of the tracks is being abused; they are much less likely to be taken seriously. It's the "poor little rich girl/boy" attitude that gives these abusers this added protection.

A bigger part of my reason for sharing my story is to help recovering *runners* to heal. You are not alone. You are not bad because you "chose" to run away from "home." Our choices were taken away early in life - and then we were labeled as a "runaway" - as if we made a decision to live a life on the streets. As if we chose to be victimized by the predators we were groomed for. We were not just runaways; if anything we were throw-aways, raised without love or care. We were abused, devalued and neglected.

The biggest reason I am sharing my story is to prove that nothing is impossible. No matter the scars, no matter how deep the wounds, there is nothing that can hold you down if you choose to forge ahead and create a life filled with happiness. We all hold the key to self-healing - and to our ultimate happiness. Where we come from serves to make us who we are - but it does not define us. We choose who we are and who we become each and every day.

2 A RUNAWAY CHILD'S BURDEN

Being lost in someone who doesn't exist is the burden that is unique to a runaway child. A runaway child never gets a sense of self or identity. We are no one. We are throw-away children at best. No home, no family and no roots or history. We manage to carry this burden well because we are purely focused on physical survival. It is a sad disconnected existence made especially tragic because we are the children who need and crave love the most. We are the children where love was a weapon to be used against us. The people charged with loving and protecting us took advantage of our desperate need to be loved as they dished out their cruelty. Those same people groomed us to be the perfect victims for predators at large. We are a predator's dream. We've been raised for them. Silent, obedient and needy. Predators give us the sense of the "love" and "belonging" that we are starved for; we do what is expected with little or no resistance in order to receive.

Once a runaway, always a runaway. That is who I am at my core. I began physically running away at the age of five. Prior to that I retreated into an imaginary world or simple numbness to get me through. To this day when the tough comes in, my tough gets going. The moment a relationship or anything in my life is going south my knee-jerk reaction is to bolt. I literally will start looking for a new place to live, usually in a new country. I cannot tell you how many times I have jumped ship this way. To outsiders I look like a brave adventurer. The sad truth is I am simply running from pain to nothingness. In fact as I write these words I am in the middle of my new country search fighting against myself and trying to stay put at the same time. If I am not planning a move to a far away land, I am at a minimum running out on an argument. Runaways don't work through relationships. We don't inherently understand how to work through even the slightest conflict. To us conflict signifies the end of the world in a very literal sense. The threat of someone not loving us, not liking us or abandoning us in any way is akin to dying a slow death by way of torture. This is also what keeps us silent and chameleon-like. We will like what you like to secure love; not because we are willfully deceptive, we do this simply because our need for love supersedes all sense or logic. Add to the mix that as runaways developing a sense of self is arrested. We have adult responsibilities, but we are far from being adults. We skip over all of the milestones where most children scrape their knees while cocooned in a safe environment. We don't get to make mistakes and have someone to guide us through to safety. There is no junior or senior high school. We never experience those normal social situations that teenagers grow through. We don't know or trust a soft place to fall. We turn everything inward and cope by running. It is all that we know.

3 ALL I NEED IS LOVE

Although I am tough, somehow I am not hard. I am a strong, walking wounded person who has made peace with most of her demons. That being said, I am still somewhat powerless in my need to be loved. I am motivated by my need for love and my need for inclusion. I will still do almost anything for love and to be loved; including sacrificing my innermost desires to feel a sense of belonging, even if it only lasts a moment. When the moment is over and it always has an end, the emotional runner takes over. I find my way inside of myself, into the compartment where numb lives. This space finds children of abuse at a very young age. I almost think I was born with it because I don't remember a time when this space didn't exist for me. The numb is my salvation.

As a small child the numb controlled me. As an adult I summon it at will. That power is the difference between survival and *surthrival*. Being in charge of this space allows me to function and redirect my energies for my good rather than being powerless and overtaken. It insulates me against depression which I am very much prone to due to my familial history. I come from a long line of maternal relatives that suffered from alcoholism, drug abuse, depression, bipolarity and borderline personality disorder.

4 THE GOOD LITTLE GIRL

The life that is apparent to on-lookers, the person that everyone has seen or currently sees... Once upon a time I was a homemaker with five children, a Mother, step-mother, wife, PTO (Parent Teacher Organization) president, room mother for four of my five children's classes simultaneously (it would have been all five except the youngest wasn't in school yet), Girl Scout leader, mentor... volunteer extraordinaire. I immersed myself in being perfect; the perfect housewife, the perfect friend that never said no. I was always dressed well and I never left my house without makeup (Mother would have been proud). I kept physically fit working out like a demon. I would stay up until midnight baking 140 cupcakes for all of my children's classes because I wouldn't do for one and not the other. You could eat off of the floors of my almost fully tiled 3700 square foot house. Everything was always in its place. My cover was perfect. So perfect in fact that even my ex-husband didn't really know who I was. This man knew most of my history and healed me through my hell of memories that I could bear to reveal to him. He was for many years my soft place to fall. Even so, I hid my true self from him. My opinion was always his opinions, period. The irrational fear that he would stop loving me kept me without an original thought.

Then there was the good little girl (She is still alive and well and we are in constant battle.)...good student, obedient, quiet and only pushing the limits within the rules of dress code as a prep-school punk rocker. As my way of being different I would wear multicoloured glittery eyeshadow and pointy toed retro pumps with my very conservative Connecticut private school uniform. This was my only rebellion against being the "Good little girl."

The good little girl is desperate for belonging. I was the daughter to anyone who would love and parent me and I was a child who belonged to no one. No one person was around long enough to claim me in a meaningful, loving way. When my mother wasn't being abusive and neglectful it was because she was absent, off to parts unknown. She was usually with a man; Sometimes she was on "holiday," in mental institution.

To on-lookers now, my friends, my family and acquaintances I am a warm, loving, insightful, intelligent, positive and at times a funny woman. An artist and freelancer in whatever I can dig my heels into. Fearless and always willing to reinvent myself. Brave and resourceful. I take these words from what I have been told. It has taken me almost fifty years to come into my own. What people see now is the real me without benefit of knowing my history. The person I am now is who I have strived to be and never believed in. I am a person who has a voice and an opinion. Gone is the girl that could not say no. I cannot tell you what the turning point was. I can tell you the turning point is constant. I still have to fight the remnants of my demons and reactions.

There have been more than a few times while in discussion with my boyfriend where I will grip the kitchen counter that I am sitting on to prevent myself from running out of his apartment. Sit I do, in discussion divulging my true opinion the consequences be damned, trembling on the inside. I can't say that I always stay put. I left my boyfriend last night as he lay sleeping. I tried to stay, I had an inner dialogue that took me back and forth between running and staying put, desperately hoping that I would fall asleep. In the morning he awoke to an empty bed. I just needed to retreat and could not fight it any longer. I am angry and frustrated with myself, but I just could not stick it out. We have a date in a couple of days and no doubt I will have to face the music. I will have to share what had me so tied in knots that caused me to take to the road. The good part of that is I know I will do it, trembling or not; and the world will not stop spinning.

I look forward to the day I no longer have to white knuckle a counter to stay put. The day where I sleep through the night and deal with the conflict in the morning. I look forward to the day my opinions flow without measuring each word so as to be overly diplomatic. It will come. I will make it so because I have something that runaway girl never had. Awareness. The awareness that my coping mechanisms are no longer necessary and that I am best served staying put, no matter the outcome. The awareness that stability comes from within and I can give it to myself. I will ultimately win out over the urge to run but until then I will forgive myself when I need to go.

5 THE ROOF OVER MY HEAD

The "home" I left was no safer than my life on the streets. Actually there were several homes. Each was pretty and had all of the essentials, plus some. Big backyards, some with pools, one on a canal leading out to Biscayne Bay. The condos were always waterfront high-rises with a view of the ocean. From the time we moved to Florida we had a live-in housekeeper that would keep me well fed and somewhat protected. My bedrooms were large and well decorated. I had a beautiful wardrobe (must keep up appearances). My bed was soft and comfy. My most prized possessions were two guitars, a flute, a keyboard and a sketch pad. Materially I wanted for nothing. Emotionally I wanted for everything. The pain and uncertainty I ran to was far less than the pain and instability I ran from. My "home" was a minefield filled with emotionally violent ambiguity. I never knew what I would come into when I returned from a day at school. Add to that, being used and abused by a stranger was much more palatable than at the hands of the people who are supposed to love and protect me.

At a minimum, once a week there was one thing I could count on; My mother on the warpath aiming at the huge bulls-eye that encompassed my entire being. No surprise that this day would most often be timed with our housekeepers day off. No witnesses and no possible protectors. There was no rhyme or reason for the attack. This was just the way it was.

It would go like this:

I would come home from school and my mother would have a look about her that would cause me to brace myself for the impending attack. In a tone that reeked with distain she would tell me to follow her to my bedroom. Between myself and the housekeeper my bedroom and everything in it was always, and I do mean always, immaculate. My mother was a compulsive neat freak. You could open any cupboard in the house and it would look like something out of the movie "Sleeping with the Enemy." Labels forward, items arranged according to size...that sort of thing. (I carried that same habit into my adulthood. I did not however, expect my children to do the same.). Nonetheless my mother would manage to find something or create something out of place. Usually the latter. Her number one move would be to go into my closet, wrinkle a perfectly folded shirt over and tear everything in my room apart whilst in a screaming rage. It...she was petrifying. She looked and acted as if she was possessed by the soul of a rabid dog.

In the midst of her tirade(s) I would stand quietly, eyes to the floor and wait for the storm to pass over. She would scream me me, attack me with the following phrases and then some; 'Look at this! Look at this mess! Slob! You are nothing but a little tramp! A user! Everyone knows you are sick in the head!' She would leave, still screaming while "slamming" the pocket door behind her as best she could without it coming off its track. I would immediately, (fearing her return for a second go-round) begin cleaning up the chaos left in her wake. I think for her this was a "kick the cat" kind of thing. I think she felt so out of control of the life around her that this was her way of gaining control; And she could and did control me.....at least on the surface.

Piece by piece I would begin to pick up the clothes; Re-hanging each item facing in the same direction, dark to light, sleeved to sleeveless, jackets, shirts top button done, dresses, skirts, pants and finally I would refold the t-shirts in her particular way, carefully replacing them onto the shelves. All the while I would be wishing her dead, imagining her murder and/or planning my run. Tears would be burning like a blazing forest fire in my eyes; Tears that dared not flow.

My mother would have you believe I was nothing more than a troubled child and that was the reason I kept running away. Indeed, she had many convinced of this. She was a terrific actress, chameleon....liar. The truth is that no child would exchange a real home for a park bench without very good reason. I did not do drugs or drink alcohol. I was an exceptionally good student. I was not a problem child. My need to fit in would not allow me to be disobedient. My fear of rejection or being in the spotlight made me visibly well-behaved. Simple teenage rebellion does not make a child live through hunger day after day for over three years. The drive to not go back 'home' and be at a minimum physically fed would take over, if for no other reason than survival.

6 THE FIVE YEAR OLD RUNAWAY

I ran away from home many, many times before it stuck. I ran away more times than I can count or recall. Beginning at the age of five, the majority of the runs were brief, ranging from a few hours up to a day or two... some were never discovered, most were. In the early years - prior to age nine - I was running to something, someone. I was trying to find my *Daddy*. I was sure that he could fix everything. I had no real recollection of him as my daddy - unless you count a hot dog and a coke in his office as fathering. He left my mother when I was barely a toddler. I tried to do the same but it proved much more difficult for a small child.

Around the age of 5 my half-brother and I went to live with my grandparents full time. My half-brother Steven, who was five and a half years my senior, was from my mother's first marriage. The year would have been 1971. Being divorced one time carried quite a stigma, never mind twice. I'm quite sure my grandmother spared no word to make my mother feel like the lowest form of life for her failures. My mother was most definitely my grandmother's one and only target. She was the oldest of three girls. Both of my aunts somehow managed to live up to my grandmother's expectations. I imagine they learned what not to do from my mother.

During my grandparent years my mother would ghost in and out for a day or two. Her visits were almost never pleasant. My grandparent's home was better than my mother's in terms of nutrition and overall physical safety. I wasn't being dropped out of two-story windows and had access to food on a regular basis. There was also a live-in au pair that acted as a buffer between my grandmother's alcoholism and my grandfather's abuse - to a degree. It's important to note that my mother wasn't born to be an abusive self-loathing individual; she was created, and now I was living with her creators. It would be many years before I realized that most people's grandmothers did not hide partially consumed drinks. I would find them with the ice barely melted behind picture frames on book shelves or under multiple bathroom sinks.

As far as the reasons my mother (whom I will from this point on address by the pseudonym *Evil One*) gave my half-brother and I over to my grandparents... Let me count the ways. She set our duplex on fire when she fell asleep with a cigarette in her hand while in a drug induced haze. She would disappear for days at a time leaving us in the care of a ten year who with no food or money would get her parents to pick us up. Oh, and then there was that time when I was five years old that she dropped me out of a two story window for financial gain. I broke both of my arms in three places.· I can still remember the sensation of the fall, and that it was drizzling out. I woke up on the grass in a fog as *Evil One* was scooping me up in a blanket, taking me via taxi to the hospital. Yes taxi, not ambulance. In the days that followed she filed suit against the landlord for not having screens on the windows. True story. Add to that the neglect. My ten year old babysitter would often find her passed out in bed as I sat in my crib so starved that I would be eating my own feces. I developed rickets due to malnutrition. I was born a perfect little body and given bowed legs as a direct result of the Evil One's neglect. I have vague memories of having a steel bar attached to my baby shoes to correct the position that my feet were in as a result of my bowed legs. I would frequently try to pull the bar off of my shoes to no avail.

The rejection by my mother resulted in the birth of 'the good little girl' that took me over. I have been told by the babysitter who witnessed these events what a good little girl I was. I am relating these stories from some of her recollections and some of my own memories. My babysitter told me that she never saw my mother hold me, or so much as smile in my direction. She said that when she'd come in to clean me up she never opened the bedroom door to a crying baby. She said, and I quote, *"It was almost as if you were afraid to cry."*

7 RUNNING TO MY DADDY

Based off of the day I went to my father's office for that memorable hot dog and coke, I knew that my Daddy was in a tall building not too far from my grandparent's house. Of course when you are six or seven *everything* is very tall..... and the moon follows you. That being said, at a minimum I knew it was a building. I would later come to realize this was the Montreal Forum, not just any building but a famous one, a landmark.

My father was the Vice President of the Forum as well as a professional bowler. He also worked closely with the Montreal Canadiens hockey team alongside my uncle who was their general manager. Because of his professions his image would appear in *The Montreal Gazette* on occasion. While he and my mother were together she created a scrapbook of clippings from the articles that he was featured in. That book lived under her bed and I would often leaf through it in secret. I would sneak into the *Evil One's* room and lay quietly on my tummy next to the bed. My mother would be passed out under the influence of alcohol and/or barbiturates as I stared wistfully at his photographs. I would imagine he was my knight in shining armor. I would picture him coming to rescue me. I would also watch him bowling on TV from time to time. This was my relationship with my father. So often I can remember wondering why he didn't like me enough to pick me up the way my brother Steven's father did. I was less than five years old and all I could do was wonder what I did wrong. I would be left with this feeling for a great many years. It wasn't until I became a mother for the third time at the age of 26 that I realized and felt that it truly wasn't anything that I did that made him leave. I can still hear my aunt telling me it was his loss, not mine. Words that echo in my soul and yet did no good. I was simply too young to grasp their meaning.

As if having my father abandon me wasn't confusing and painful enough, I watched in wounded envy as my brother Steven enjoyed a relationship with his father. I would grow up with the knowledge that some fathers love their children and show up... at least some of the time.

Every other weekend Steven and I would sit on the stoop outside of my grandparent's house and wait for his father to arrive. There were the times when Steven's father was a no-show. No notice, no phone call, at least none that we were made aware of. Something tells me there was a phone call, but that my alcoholic grandmother couldn't be bothered to let him know. We would sit in silence as he stared at the road in wait. Sometimes we would sit from morning until dusk, with no one coming out to retrieve us.

When he did show up, I would be there waiting with Steve, hoping his Daddy would take me along as well. Once in a blue moon he did. But mostly I would just sit and watch as Steven climbed into his Daddy's car. I would feel abandoned and alone as they drove off on what I imagined would be some great adventure. The kind of adventure saved for good children, not children like me. This was a further validation that I must have done something really horrible to not have my father come and pick me up the way that my half-brother's father did.

Still, I never gave up trying. Most of my runs to find my father originated from my Grandparent's house. I would walk from their place toward the tall buildings in the distance. I was certain that I could find my daddy's office. Five, six, seven, eight and nine years old, I would run; returning to their home before dark, avoiding discovery much of the time. Somewhere inside of me I was sure if I could just show up he would have to keep me, even if he didn't like me (as if he wouldn't know where to return me). There were occasions where my timing was off and I wouldn't make dusk, aka curfew. Had I known where I was going I would have made it with time to spare; it turns out the forum was only a little over 2 kilometres from my front door.

One of those days that I didn't make curfew inspired me to make a big change in my runaway routine. I was seven years old and it struck me that trying to get there on foot was what was holding me back. With this in mind I determined that a bus was a much smarter way to get to the tall buildings. I scraped together 10 cents - money I would normally use to buy my favourite Black Cat bubblegum - and used it to board a bus. I had so much confidence that I would make it to my daddy that buying a return ticket was of no concern to me. I took a seat by the window. I sat with my hopeful little seven year old face pressed against the glass, watching as the bus passed through my suburban neighbourhood toward the tall buildings. As I gazed out the window, the bus stopping and starting as it let people on and off, I fell asleep. I don't know how long I was on the bus, I can only estimate. I boarded after school so probably 2:00 pm and hours later... maybe ten or eleven at night, I was awakened by the driver at the final stop.

To this day it boggles my mind how the bus driver allowed me to exit the bus without concern or question. Let me off he did, this tiny little girl brushing four feet tall at best, late at night, in the dark, in the middle of a residential neighbourhood that I didn't recognize. The neighbourhood was barely lit by street-lamps and there were no tall buildings in sight. As I began walking, unease set in.... and then numb... a total separation of body and self. No thoughts that I can recall... I walked with no direction.

Fortunately for me a couple walking a German Shepherd noticed this lost looking little girl. I immediately took to them and their dog. Having had a German Shepherd of my own I felt a sense of comfort, even kinship to these complete strangers. The couple invited me back to their home and offered me a Coke. Coca Cola was a big treat for me back then, I always remember the special occasions when I was allowed to have one. As I sat sipping my soda pop they called the police and were able to return me to my grandparents.

I imagine that my grandparents' relief was great but, I couldn't tell. The anger was all that I could see, feel or understand. My grandfather was shouting questions at me. "Why did you get on a bus? Where were you going? What were you thinking?" I remember him telling me that if I lied he would know because he could read the lines on my forehead. I believed him. I can picture myself touching my bangs to see if they were in position so as to obscure the view of my forehead.

As a child who learned to be silent early on I never disclosed why I ran, or even that I ran at all. In fact I did not utter so much as one word. I just stood there, stoic in my black school tunic, silky thin chestnut hair brushing the tops of my brows, tears stinging the backs of my glassy green eyes. In that moment I swore to myself to make damn sure that I always returned home before dusk as I continued my search for my daddy.

8 THE EVIL ONE'S VISITS

During the years I lived with my grandparents E.O. would come and go with no defined rhythm. I know from overheard conversations that she spent time in a mental institution. I also remember her having bandages taken off of slashed, healed wrists with no idea of what had occurred to give her such awful boo boos. I know she also spent a great deal of time partying and husband hunting. This was a woman raised to be dependent on a man. She had no love for herself let alone any belief that she should or could stand on her own. This was a woman who had nothing to give one child, let alone two. She ran on empty doing her best to fill her own hollowness. She was a woman who suffered mental illness at a time when mental illness wasn't cool. Not that it's cool now. But back then we were only just becoming aware of psychology. If you went to counseling people assumed there was something really wrong with you. It simply was not socially acceptable, even less so in a family like mine. Wealthy people didn't suffer mental illness, period.

I only have a few snap shot memories of E.O. during my grandparent house years. Sometimes she would pick only my brother up and take him to a concert or snow skiing. I would cry when they would leave together not understanding why she wasn't taking both of us at the same time. I realize now that with our age difference, taking me to an Isacc Hayes concert would not have been enjoyable for Steven or I. But as a five year old who hadn't seen her mother for long periods all I knew was that she was leaving me behind. On the visits where she would pick only me up it would be to go shopping, or she would take me to little modelling jobs for a clothing line. I remember once the owner who was also a family friend told me I could pick out any outfit I wanted and keep it. I excitedly looked through the aisles and aisles of dresses in this huge wholesale warehouse. I finally settled on a dark blue faux denim dress with giant grommets all over it. Very 70s. E.O. hated it and tried to get my attention elsewhere but the owner saw me select the dress so she was powerless to veto my pick. She stood there glaring at me and I knew it would be trouble. I knew I should have put it back and acted like it wasn't my real pick. But I loved that dress, I wanted it more than I cared about my mother's wrath in that moment. In a very unusual moment of bravery… or stupidity, I held onto the dress, consequences be damned.

The car ride home was a long and painful one, words like *stupid, tramp, ugly, follower, user and people don't like little girls who talk too much* took up most of the space. She dropped me off and it was a long time before her next visit.

There were also a few times I was happy to see my mother. Well actually, initially I was always happy to see her. At first sight I would somehow forget what a horribly cold and frightening person she was. The happy would evaporate immediately during the initial moments of her walking through the front door. After a coaxed greeting, my eyes would hit the floor and I would stand silently listening to what the plan was. My pick-up or Steven's or maybe it was a Jewish holiday family get-together visit. The family/friends occasion visits were my favourite. It meant being with Evil One in public. She was a great mother/performer given an audience. Oscar award worthy. She might even hold my hand for a moment to look the part. I knew how to work those moments. Like a sponge I would absorb any affection she would pass my way. It would also be during these moments that I would learn that she could control her behaviour. She could choose to be kind. She could choose to be loving. But she didn't, not unless she had an audience to play for. To this day I cannot reconcile why. I am sure I never will.

Occasionally she would stay a night or two. On the visits that she would stay overnight she would sleep in her childhood bedroom. If I was particularly lucky and she was in a good mood, I would get a rare treat. As long as I promised to stay still and quiet she would let me come into her room. I used to love that room. She never knew that I snuck in when she was gone. I was smart enough not to disturb anything so I never got caught. Her room had a vanity dressing table that was filled with makeup. I never touched any of the makeup, but I would play make-believe and imagine myself dolled up like a princess. I can picture myself pointing at the eyeshadow, pretending to apply it, and then the blush... point and apply, and finally, the lipstick. As if I had magic little fingers.

I treasured the times she let me in there, watching as she readied herself for a date, a night out, or to leave altogether. I would sit quiet as a church mouse in awe of her expertise. It seems all of Evil One's beauty was saved for the exterior. She was a striking beauty by everyone's account. When my mother entered a room no one was immune. She stood around 5'7, slim with natural double D's. She had long silky raven hair which cascaded to the middle of her back, and full lips that women these days go to cosmetic surgeons to achieve. Dark brown, almost black almond shaped eyes, olive skin and high cheekbones. She looked to be a cross of Italian and Native American descent. She could have been the offspring of Sophia Loren, Linda Gray and Cher combined. As for her style she was always ahead of the curve, and knew very well how to dress her own. She took great pride in her appearance. Sadly this was the only thing she felt she had to offer. No one could draw a man in better than my mother; and no one could scare him off further than my mother.

It was fear that made my father leave, fear for his life. I would learn this in my forties when I finally established a relationship with him.

9 MY BRAND NEW DADDY

After a few years of being in my grandparents "care" my mother arrived with a brand new Daddy. His name was Alvin Leonard Finkelstein. Prior to my mother people called him Al or Alvin. Evil One did not approve of either of those names; she insisted on Lenny. That should have been his first clue as to what he was in for. A controlling crazy woman. Who insists on a person changing their name? Who actually agrees to it? Answer: a man swept into her beauty and apparently magical vagina. No joke.

I could not tell you when her last visit was, I could only say that it had been a long time. I was eight almost nine years old by now, and prior to the introduction to my new Father the Evil One pulled me aside. She held my arm and said "Behave, don't talk too much, and call him Daddy." Not seeing my mother for extended periods did not fade my memory of what her wrath felt like. The fear was autonomic, a part of my being, deeply imbedded in my soul. Time did nothing to fade my knowledge that to survive my mother, obeying without question was essential. I also knew that I was about to go live with her full-time. Being in any way disobedient would not have served me well. As she spoke I peered around her to see what my new Daddy looked like. He had a kind face, not particularly handsome but also not un-attractive. Short brown curly hair, the result of a perm that was in style back then. Happy blue eyes and a bit of a belly that I would later refer to as my pillow. He was a big man, quite tall... I'm thinking over 6 feet.

Per my mother's direction I went and sat dutifully next to her new man on the plastic covered sofa in my grandparent's immaculate parlor. This was the kind of room that you passed on the way to the living room, the kind of room that was to be admired and not used. Entry was only allowed on special occasions, which would inevitably be followed by the use of the "good" china at dinner. I loved that room because it had a piano. It took all the self control I had not to sneak in to play it. When my grandparents would take their big yearly trip to Europe for a month, I would play it. I would make sure the housekeeper was in her room, thinking she wouldn't hear me. Looking back I'm sure she did. Her name was Norma, and she was the best. She allowed my brother and me to have new pets when my grandparents went on vacation. The only conditions were that we never tell and that we get rid of them before they returned. In total we had mice, a turtle and a salamander . Unfortunately, the mice escaped and the salamander died. The turtle threw us under the bus. He escaped on the day my grandparents were due back and we couldn't find him anywhere; regrettably, my grandmother did. Turns out he was in the pocket of her silk robe. Bye-bye rodent and reptilian pets forever.

Okay, back to my new daddy. Lenny smiled at me as I sat, immediately taking my hand. His hands were huge; he was like a giant to me... a big, kind, soft giant. Being the obedient (good little girl) child that I was, I, without missing a beat, said "Daddy can I have a pony?" No joke, I remember it clear as day. Funny thing is, as much as I love horses I don't remember pining for a pony in such a way that it would even make sense for this to be my first request. Looking back I can almost hear him chuckling at my request. I fell for him in that moment of laughter, hook, line and sinker.

My new Daddy turned out to be an absolute g-dsend for me. He made me his Daddy's girl from the moment he took my little hand. This Daddy filled the void and made many things better. The only thing I was upset about was my having to take on a new last name. I had just learned how to sign my name in cursive on my library card. Signing that library card marked the beginning of being big enough to take home books. It was a really big deal to me, so much so that I can remember being really put out. The eight letters in Grundman took what seemed almost an eternity to master well enough to be accepted by the librarian. Now my new last name, Finkelstein had eleven letters. To my nine year old self it was an insurmountable task. I didn't realize at the time that a new daddy also meant a new school, with new rules and a new country where as it turned out a library card would be much easier to attain.

I would quickly forget about the school library as I settled into having my very own new daddy. He gave me the love that I had craved and made me feel safe. Having my very own daddy brought most of my running to a halt. Which was a good thing since to run back to my other Daddy I would have had to run from Miami to Montreal. No doubt I would have found a way to stow away on an airplane.

As we settled into Florida, life was becoming a beach. As I am an Aquarius and a true water baby it was the perfect place for me. I loved the ocean and swimming pool. Life was better than pretty good. Evil One would even travel from time to time leaving my Daddy and I to have actual fun. He wasn't allowed to cook when she was home, she complained he made too much of a mess. Never mind that the housekeeper would clean up after. He was an amazing cook and even let me help. This would usually be the first thing we did upon her departure. He made the best Shrimp Creole I have ever had, even to this day. There were a couple of times he took me to Disney World in secret. We went with Evil One once; hell is not a strong enough word for how that trip went.

My runs were rare at this point, saved for times when my Daddy was away on business. Times when I was left unprotected and alone with the Evil One.

10 ALL GOOD THINGS MUST COME TO AN END

All good things must come to an end, a life lesson I learned very early on life. I only had my new daddy for three years. Tragically he died two weeks after my twelfth birthday.

I came home from school to find my father's car in the driveway. He wasn't usually home until later in the evening and I was excited to see him. As I ran into his bedroom room to say hi, I was stunned at the sight of him... and the sound. He was lying partially face-down in his suit with his feet hanging of the off of the bed, and he was snoring; I had heard my father snore before, but this was different. The sound was deafeningly loud, and gurgly (I would later learn that this was not a snore, it was a death rattle. It was the sound of a man dying.). My father was a meticulous man. He always changed and hung his work clothes up when he came home He was certainly not the type of man that would lie around in his suit. As I approached the bed my mother (She had been on vacation for three weeks, my father was home because he had picked her up from the airport.) rushed out of the bathroom and shooed me out of the bedroom. She had one finger to her lips and the other pointing to the hallway; I followed her to the kitchen in silence. She leaned against the counter and pointed to a bottle of gin so as to insinuate that he was passed out, drunk. I cannot ever recall my father drinking to pass-out excess; EVER. Let alone in the middle of the day. After a moment my mother spoke, "we are leaving daddy, he's not making any money." I can remember thinking that there was no way I was going to leave him. I can also remember being paralyzed and trembling with fear. I said nothing. I went to my room, guilt-ridden for not standing up for my daddy. I shut the door, slid down the wall and sat, tears stinging the backs of my eyes until they gave way to my numb.

I was still sitting on the floor of my bedroom trying to make sense of what was happening when my brother came home. Within moments I could hear him telling my mother that my father was blue and not breathing. He told my mother that they needed to call 911. I could hear her arguing with him, but he ignored her and called. The paramedics came and opened my bedroom door to take my father out on a gurney. My mother kept yelling for them to close my door, but the hallway was tight and they needed my door open to take him out of the house. You may think she was just trying to protect me from seeing my father in that condition. The truth is she was trying to hide me from when the police showed up to take a report.

The last time I saw my father he had a machine on his chest as he was being loaded into an ambulance. My mother sent me to Sindy's house and told me she would call me from the hospital. I wanted to go with my father, but the choice was not mine. I didn't hear from my mother that night. My father had been in the hospital before and I never imagined that he would not be coming home. I went to sleep thinking that he would be fine. It never entered my mind that he could die...

In the morning my grandfather called to tell me to go home. As I walked in the door my mother through her crocodile tears stated "Your Daddy is dead." I remember with great clarity wishing with all of my heart that it had been her. For years, I felt and carried tremendous guilt that I had not spoken up for him in the kitchen. I remember feeling that she killed him, I did not know how, but I knew she did.

Fast forward ten plus years after my father's death; I came across the police and autopsy report from that day. The police never interviewed me. They never knew I had been in the house. My mother and brother banned together and made sure I would never be questioned. I say they banned together, but to be fair I am sure my brother followed whatever my mother demanded, just as we all did. They both lied and stated that they were the only ones in the house. The autopsy found no alcohol in his bloodstream. His death was ruled a suicide, caused by an overdose of Diabinese (a drug used to control diabetes). My father had been taking the Diabinese at least a year without incident. My mother had my father's body cremated; it was her good luck that cremation had been his wish.

As if my father's passing was not enough, within a few weeks I came home to find out that my mother had given away my German Shepherd. My dog, Gucci (my mother named her) was a gift from my daddy. My mother gave her away with no explanation or warning. She told me that she sent Gucci to live with a family in the country. That was it. Gucci was gone. My beautiful dog was more than just my best friend, sometimes she was my only friend. She was my confidant. She knew ALL of my secrets. She was my comfort when my daddy was out of town. There were many times she kept me from running away because I didn't want to leave her behind with my mother.

With my father and dog gone my running ways returned in full force, with one big difference. I was no longer running to my old daddy. Now, I was simply running to escape the Evil One. I was also not concerned with returning by dusk - or ever.

Left at the mercy of the Evil One I would run away several times over the course of four years before it finally stuck. Most times the police would be called and find me within a few hours. On occasion I would be gone a day or two and return on my own, either out of fear of discovery or because I had nowhere to go.

Sometimes I would run to a nearby field and hide in the trees, I loved climbing trees. I was quite a tomboy and had the scraped knees to prove it. Sometimes I hid in my "boyfriend" Robert's house; I was 12 and he was fourteen so barely boyfriend. A few of the times I ran I would break into my best friend Sindy's house and hide in her closet; sometimes unbeknownst to her, sometimes known.

On one of the runs when I hid in Sindy's house I almost gave the poor thing a heart attack. I was whispering out to her from her closet to let her know that I was there. I didn't realize that she had already fallen asleep. She woke up and thought there was a ghost in her bedroom; she immediately began screaming out for her mom. Poor thing. I felt terrible for scaring her.

I thought Sindy's mom would be angry with me, but as it turned out she felt really bad for me. She told me that she had to call the Evil One, but would see if I could at least finish out the night at her house. Even though she had no idea what I was running from she acted for my protection. Maybe Sindy broke my confidences and shared some of what I told her. At any rate E.O. was not about to let me spend the night. Can't say as I blame her. With each run I was outing her, and feeding her anger. Appearances were everything to her. We had to look like the perfect little family. Everything had to be expensive and impeccable. We even had designer mommy daughter outfits to prove how "close" we were. My runs served to shine a spotlight that all wasn't as it seemed. Looking back my runs were obviously a cry for help. If I had wanted to stay gone I would have. I purposely ran for short periods. I think I was hoping that I would be sent to live with the aunt who was always trying to save me. That might have been an option if I gave the authorities the information that they needed to help me. Unfortunately, I was too frightened to tell. I just knew I would not be believed, or taken seriously.

There were many times when the police would be the ones to locate me. So many in fact that a few of the officers knew who I was.

On one of my runs the police found me at Robert's house. I had hidden there undiscovered a few times prior and he, like Sindy was always on my side. Normally I would only stay until his parents came home. I would then either end up going back to my house or to a field.

On what would be the last time I used Robert's house as a safe -house I ended up hiding underneath his bed. Robert's mother arrived home early and we could hear her speaking to the police at their front door. We listened as they made their way down the hall and in desperation, I flew under his bed. I watched their feet, daring not to breathe as they questioned Robert. As I held my breath, I could hear my heart beating out of my chest. Evidently so could they. One of the policemen got onto his knees and began coaxing me out. "It's okay, nobody is going to hurt you. Why don't you come out and talk to us? Your Mom is really worried about you." What a scene; and what a joke; "Your Mom is really worried about you." It makes me laugh to look back on it. I don't know why exactly. I guess I am taking pleasure in the balls I had in the face of it all. Those cries for help took guts. I was terrified of my mother, yet I would run away with regularity; consequences be dammed. I am sure it was this same ballsiness that enabled me to survive the streets during the three plus year run.

The police would always ask why I ran away. They were trying to help me, but I knew they couldn't - and ultimately wouldn't - if they found out the real truth. As they would question me, the child of silence would take centre stage. Glassy green eyes on floor accompanied by shrugging shoulders. What could I say? I had no physical scars to prove that I was being tortured. From the outside we were an upper middle class family, we had a live-in who took care of me and the house. What could possibly be wrong? I was no longer being starved, I was well groomed; and again NO visible scars on my body. Add to that the fact that I believed I was at fault. I believed I was defective, bad. I had been brainwashed to believe that I deserved the treatment I was receiving.

There were a few times - very few - that I confided in one of my aunts. Well intentioned she would try to counsel E.O. or she would recommend that I see a therapist. E.O's translation? She would say "Your Aunt thinks you're sick and need a shrink. I'm going to take you and everyone will know how sick you are;" OR "Oh so you're telling your aunt made-up stories? You think she actually believes you? You are just a sick little tramp (my pet name beginning around the age of seven). Nobody will ever believe you." I figured if my own Aunties believed that I was sick then the police would certainly lock me up and throw away the key; and so the silence lived on, cemented in place.

11 SERIAL ESCAPE ARTIST

As a serial runner there were periods of time wherein my runs would become dormant. No trauma = no running. In the four months following my Daddy's death my running was anything but dormant. The running was as out of control as my mother's rages. Fortunately, summer came and I went to Montreal... far, far away from the Evil One.

Evil One remarried four months after my Daddy's passing. So much for a year of *Shiva* (a period of mourning in the Jewish religion; widows are not supposed to shop for new clothes, dance, celebrate, let alone date, etc., for a period of one year.). I was in Montreal staying with my aunt and uncle while attending a day camp until sleep-away camp began. A couple of weeks into my stay Evil One called to excitedly announce her re-marriage. Apparently I was meant to have known the man as he was an acquaintance of my Daddy. I had no memory of him. As far as I was concerned I had never met this man and had no idea what I would be returning "home" to. As if that wasn't bad enough this phone call also marked the beginning of my mourning process. When my Daddy died I didn't believe it. I sat at the funeral and while I knew someone was in the pine box set for cremation I didn't believe it was my Daddy. I believed he would never leave me. I believed his love for me would not allow him to die. This night, this phone call, marked the moment my grief; the floodgates of my mourning would begin. My aunt tried to get me to talk, but I knew better. I knew that any words spoken would make it back to my mother thus creating a wrath-filled consequence. I cried myself to sleep that night, and then awake. I cried for many more nights after that until I had no moisture left in my body to form a tear.

In the four months after my step-father's death I had met a few of Evil One's suitors. I wondered for the rest of the summer if this new father would be like any of them. One night during one of her husband hunting evenings she stumbled into my room drunk, with some guy named Dave. I loved when she was lightly drunk. She was warm and would show me affection. My mother woke me up and introduced me to this man en-route to her bedroom. I remember him vividly even though I never saw him again. He was old with a full head of long white hair and bronzed leathery skin. He wore a button-down shirt with far few buttons fastened. His hairy grey chest on full display and adorned with a plethora of gold chains, one with a massive coin on it. You might wonder how it is I have such vivid recall of a moment that literally lasted a moment. It isn't the impact that Dave made. It was one of the few times my mother demonstrated some sort of pride in me. She was showing me off and I reveled in that feeling of her love and pride. I needed her love and approval the way a flower needs water. Normally she only had a few gears where I was concerned; distant, cold, rage-filled and nasty. The moments of love only came within an alcohol induced state or a social performance.

12 THE DEATH OF TWO FATHERS

In the wake of accepting the death of my daddy I suffered another loss. The loss of my "real" Daddy. I was at day camp when I heard a radio announcer mention my father's name. Hearing it made drew my attention immediately. I was with a group of kids and it was all I could hear, as if there was no background noise from the children surrounding me. I thought something had happened to him and freaked out running over to one of my friends in the group to ask if he had heard it. He didn't, but knew the name of the station. We went to the payphone and he helped me find the number in the phone book. "Hello, my name is Marnie Grundman, I heard you mention my father's name, Gerry Grundman on the radio. Is he ok? Can you tell me what happened?" The person on the other end started laughing and repeatedly asked "Is this a joke? Who are you really?" I hung up the phone with tears of frustration and fear burning to fall. Erny, my camp friend suggested I go to the Forum. I left camp without permission, with his directions to guide me. I showed up to the Forum and approached the receptionist behind the tall partition, speaking to her through the hole in the plexiglass. I said "My name is Marnie Grundman and I would like to see my father please." She was visibly stunned and uncomfortable. "Let me see if he is in." She picked up the phone and spoke too quietly for me to hear. Upon hanging up the phone, "He is in a conference and will not be available for the rest of the afternoon." "I can wait." I sat down and stared at my shoes patiently waiting for him to be done. I watched as she left for the day and as the cleaners came in to vacuum and empty the garbage bins. My brother showed up seemingly out of nowhere, took my hand and we walked to my aunt's house in silence. We never spoke of that day. No one spoke of that day. It was as if it had never happened. I pretended it never happened. I took comfort in the numb and went on.

13 DADDY #3

My new stepfather, Myron Topper, now answering to Mike per my mother's not so request, turned out to be an incredibly nice man. I have to hand it to Evil One, she had a knack for finding, renaming and marrying really nice "Daddies." As summer ended I returned to Florida and to my new home which happened to be conveniently located in the same neighbourhood. In addition to my new Daddy I also had yet another new last name. This time a name change wasn't accompanied by tragedy; I was no longer worried about library cards. Per my mother's need to look like the perfect *Leave it to Beaver* family she instructed me to call my new step-father, Daddy.

The thought of calling another man Daddy made me feel so incredibly disloyal. I loved my Daddy so much and had only just met this new father; add to that I wasn't nine anymore. I was twelve, and I had an opinion. Of course, true to form that opinion remained in my brain. Mike sensed my unease and said "Why don't you call me Pop? That's what my boys call me." I remember thinking this man gets it and me. He recognized what E.O. chose to ignore. He recognized the pain in my eyes and knew that people/ parents aren't just interchangeable titles. What he hadn't learned yet was that you did not refuse my mother. She was the final, the only word and she wasn't having it; "Pop" was too déclassé for her. I decided to call him Dad instead of Daddy. That was my way of holding my late step-father in a separate place and E.O. never picked up on it. Subtle rebellion, that's how I rolled.

From this point on I will refer to Mike as Pop just to keep the confusion at a manageable low. In Pop I found an ally. I was protected and the running was reduced to a new low. It wouldn't be long before he figured out that he had married a monster. He would learn to fear her and I would become his part-time confidant. One day on a car ride home from school he told me she had gone ballistic and kicked his glasses off of his face. He showed me the glasses which were bent right down the middle. The bridge of his nose had a shallow gash. "I don't know what happened, she just lost it. She went crazy and starting grabbing, kicking and hitting me." He was relating what had happened in such a way as to try to make sense of her actions. His presentation of the glasses was his proof. How lucky he was to have some sort of physical proof. Evil One was either getting sloppy or simply didn't care. I had no external reaction; we finished the ride home in a cloud of somber silence.

14 THE RUN THAT ALMOST BROKE ME

While my running was at a new low, it hadn't stopped. The last run before the three year escape was life changing. I have no memory of what made me run that day I only know that one of my aunts was in town and it was around Christmas. I think I ran because I wanted my aunt to know things were not okay. I have a sense of that, but I cannot grab onto the why. This was the aunt that was always pushing for therapy. She was also the only person in my family to ever tell me that she was proud of me and even write it in a card once. I often wished that she was my mother.

By this time I was a city bus pro. I knew the routes well, and would take the bus with my friends to the skating rink or the mall. My mother had taken my babysitting earnings from my jewelry box (for "safekeeping," I never saw it again.) and I had little more than bus fare in my pocket when I decided to run to a mall downtown. I imagine that I chose it because it was familiar territory and I knew it stayed open late. The mall had an arcade with a carousel and some other rides. I hung around the carousel watching kids with their parents, no particular thought in mind. No goal. It was just peaceful to not be at "home."

As the hours passed and the arcade area emptied, I noticed an attractive young man, maybe in his early twenties, staring at me. He was smiling at me as he walked over and began talking to me. He introduced himself and asked if I had a place to go. A predator. I did well with predators. I was, after all, groomed for them. I had been a victim of incest from a very young age. At the age of nine I had also been molested by a life guard at one of the buildings we lived in, in Miami. I couldn't spot a predator, but they could easily pick me out of a crowd.

I told the man, his name was Louis, that I had no place to go. He asked if I was hungry and of course I was. I hadn't eaten since breakfast and it was now somewhere around 11 at night. Louis's appearance gave me no cause for concern. He looked nothing like "the boogeyman," or what a twelve year old would think a boogeyman should look like. He was dressed in jeans and a button down with a light jacket. He had sandy blond hair that brushed the collar of his shirt, blue eyes and a little five o'clock shadow. I liked his attention and more-over I liked that he was going to take care of me. Or I thought I did.

We got into his car and he said he had something to show me before we grabbed a bite to eat. He drove me to an area near Haulover Beach and we proceeded to walk into a wooded area dense with sea grape trees. Like a lamb to slaughter I was completely unaware. I didn't even notice that he had a blanket in his hands. As we walked deeper in I felt a sense of fear wash over me. Before I could really identify or react to this feeling he spun me around and was sticking his tongue down my throat. By this age I had made-out with boys, but in a childlike way... the making out I had experienced was pressing lips together with closed mouths. I had no real understanding of what a boy's need or intention would be. The boys I kissed were my age; I think they barely knew their own intention.

The molestation I had experienced didn't start this way and didn't end in penetration. I had nothing to draw on. I was terrified, overwhelmed and confused. The next thing I knew he was pulling my jeans down and pushing me onto the blanket. As he began to penetrate me I was telling him it hurt, please stop. I don't know how many times I begged him to stop until I finally lay there frozen with silent tears staining my cheeks. He raped me vaginally and anally multiple times throughout the night. I never fought. I never screamed. I didn't even try to get away. I just complied. I wasn't even there. Numb; with the exception of my physical self. How I wish I could have numbed my body from the physical pain.

As if nothing out of the ordinary had occurred we got dressed as the sun had began to rise, and he took me to eat. We went to a Sambo's, a 24 hour American style diner. I ate in a fog as he talked and acted like nothing had happened. I could not tell you one word he said beyond telling me that we were running out on the check. He instructed me to go outside and wait by the car which I dutifully did. Ironically, I had no run left in me. As if the night hadn't been strange enough he then drove me home and watched as I walked into my house. It hadn't even occurred to me that he now knew where I lived.

As I walked into the house my raging mother was standing in wait. My aunt behind her, thank g-d. Buffer. She was screaming at me "Who do you think you are? Who the fuck do you think you are?!" I had no answer. Eyes on the floor, my body hurt, silence. She sent me to my room. I remember crawling un-showered into my bed, no tears... just exhausted. I passed out, numb.

A few days later Louis was back. I was jogging and he was trying to get me into his car. I made the excuse that my parents were waiting for me and he made me promise to meet him after they went to sleep. A promise I broke. The next day he was at my school. He must have been laying in wait, watching and stalking me. I never told him where I went to school.

He was on the sidewalk hanging onto the chain link fence, staring at me.

I was waiting my turn to play dodgeball, hoping he would go away or at least stay on the outside of the fence. My gym teacher noticed him and asked if me I knew him. I lied and said no. She had one of the male gym teachers go over and talk to him. Thankfully that was the last I saw of Louis.

Throughout the rest of my childhood I never told anyone in my family about the rape. Actually I didn't even know that I had been raped, I didn't have that word in my vocabulary. I was also unaware that I had lost my virginity, another word I didn't have in my vocabulary. I did know that I did something wrong. It was my fault. I didn't fight. I didn't run. I got in the car with him. I also knew without a doubt that I had proved my mother right; I was a tramp.

I would learn the word virgin and rape from my first real boyfriend, Ernesto. I met Ernesto in boarding school and it was not love at first sight, at least not for me. He would stare at me in the cafeteria and not make any effort to speak to me. It was weeks before he finally asked my roommate if I liked him. Like him? I had never spoken to him! Poor guy was not just shy, English was his second language and he didn't always feel comfortable using it in those early days. Somehow we ended up dancing together at the first school dance and that was it. From that evening on we were inseparable. We were officially a couple. This would mark the first and only period of my life where I was allowed to live as an innocent; the only time I was truly carefree.

The first time we made love Ernesto asked me why I wasn't a virgin. He then explained what that word meant. As I told him what had happened that night at Haulover beach, he couldn't believe I didn't understand what had really happened. He supported and helped me to realize that what had been done to me was not my fault. Regardless I still felt like damaged goods. His words as loving as they were only helped me to feel a little less dirty. Ernesto never knew about the earlier violations. He never knew how dirty and damaged I really was; or thought I was.

It would be ten years before I told anyone in my family about that day. The day I decided I was going to tell all, my first call was to my brother Steven. As I began to tell him what had happened he repeated one word over and over again. *"Liar."* That was that. Steven was most definitely my mother's son. He was the only one in the family I told and it went no further for obvious reasons. I truly believed that my brother would believe me... he broke what was left of my heart that day. I knew if he didn't believe me, no one would. Not ever.

15 MY HOME AWAY FROM "HOME"

In the summer following Evil One's marriage I received a postcard while at sleep away camp. It was to inform me that we were moving to Manhattan and I would be attending boarding school in Connecticut or New Jersey. While most children were receiving care-packages filled with their favourite sweets along with notes of parental affection, I was receiving life changing news. Evil One typically sent two or three post cards throughout my two month stays at summer camp. She visited on family day one time in the four years that I attended sleep-away camp. I can't say that I was unhappy about her lack of contact. I felt lonely watching the other kids with their parents. At the same time it was a relief to not have her there. I also cannot say I was unhappy with the news of boarding school. Living at summer camp was great and I figured anything was better than her house. My brother attended a military boarding school and had done really well. My only trepidation was that my school would also be military and have no music program. I played flute and was second chair at my junior high. This was my only tangible validation that I was good at something. I loved playing in the band. I was proud of it and was very upset at the thought of giving my chair up.

I tested for two schools, Hun Academy in Princeton, New Jersey and Cheshire Academy in Cheshire, Connecticut. As it turned out Hun had a music program. Cheshire academy had no band and no music program at all. I had aspirations of going to Julliard as a flautist: a school with no music program would mean the end of that dream for sure. Evil One knew nothing about my Julliard dream. She was not aware or interested in any of my aspirations. Unfortunately, I made the mistake of telling her that I wanted to attend Hun. After the interview there she informed me on the drive back to the city that I had not been accepted. She said the headmaster told her that I talked too much. It would be years before I found out that she had lied. Pop didn't know I wanted to go there and unwittingly made a comment about my choosing Cheshire over Hun. I can't say I was surprised that my mother had lied. In her eyes, if I excelled at something it proved that I was good and she was bad. That's how she operated. It was a huge relief to know that I was accepted by Hun, I carried that rejection with me for years. I am fighting not to shred her in my writing in this moment. This is why I have to call her Evil One, it is my only way to lash out without losing my mind as I relive moments like these.

16 CHESHIRE ACADEMY: MY SAFE PLACE

As E.O and Pop dropped me off at boarding school I felt a great sense of relief. She would now be two hours away by train, and longer still, by car. I had received the gift of a physical buffer.

The middle school dorm was a large house with several bedrooms upstairs. We had dorm parents who lived on the main floor of the house; they were also teachers at the school. The year I attended there were five or six live-in students. I was the only one with a roommate, and as it turned out she was a kindred spirit. My roommate Kym had already been in residence for a couple of years and knew the ropes. More importantly, as we began to unpack our bags and tape our posters on the walls over our beds, we turned to find out that had the same Cheap Trick poster! Meant to be; she was my instant new best friend.

Life at boarding school was my first taste of normal beyond my aunts' houses. But for the typical trials and tribulations of adolescence, it was virtually drama free. Every day the same. There was no one raging when I came through the door, nor would there ever be. I slept without fear of victimization. I was for the first time in my life, a carefree child. Even when E.O would attempt to mind-fuck me on the telephone I knew I was safe. I would only visit the city a handful of weekends and she was barely around when I was in. Eventually she would return to Miami and I would either visit with Pop or friends of our family.

My dorm parents were terrific and I liked the majority of my teachers. I did school well, I always liked school. I was the editor and illustrator of our middle school newsletter/paper. I also managed the boy's soccer team. After school we would go to a cool little local pizza joint that had individual jukeboxes in each booth. We'd get a coke and a slice of pizza, if we had extra cash we would splurge for a whole pie; dessert would be an ice cream cone at the local parlour. The town was small and didn't have much, but it had everything a teenager could want. On the weekends we would go to the movies or skiing. On campus we had dances and a recreation room complete with pool tables. In the spring there was a pond that Ernesto and I would frequently walk to. We would lie on a boulder in the middle of a golden dandelion filled field planning our future in between kisses.

My dorm parents had a little girl that my dorm-mates and I would babysit from time to time. Mostly we would just hang out on their floor and play with her. Occasionally they would have us over for family dinners. I of course latched on to them and decided they were my parents even though I addressed her as Mrs. and him as Coach. In addition to him being the science teacher, he coached the male sports teams. I was having the time of my life. Life was good. I had found my safe place. I had found my home.

17 THE NEGATIVE SIDE OF PERSPECTIVE

Up until my 13th year on this planet I thought everyone lived the way I did. By this time I had lived in eight different residences in four different cities with three different fathers plus my grandparents. As if that's not enough I had also had my last name changed three times. There were a couple of families, including one of my aunts' houses, that I wished that I had been a part of, but I didn't really know how different my house was on a daily basis. I thought my life was normal. I thought pain and people abandoning you was normal. It was my normal. Living in a home, a real home for the first time shined a glaring light on the hell I had been living in. Once I crossed the threshold of peace and stability, I could not willingly go back to war. The bubble had burst and now I knew better. So begins the three and a half year run.

18 MY LIFE ON THE ROAD

Day One: As I try to remember what time of year it was I am already struggling with the timeline of Day One. I think that it was around the end of the school year. That's the trick of trauma. Time is foggy. At any rate, I was thirteen when I snapped.

My mother had given me an ultimatum about returning to school and the answer was not what she expected. She knew Ernesto would factor heavily into my decision, and used him accordingly. Ernesto only had one year left until he moved on to university and I had four years until graduation.

My options were: Returning to Cheshire until my graduation which would leave me without Ernesto for three years as he went off to university; or come "home" and only be without him for a year as she believed that he was planning to attend the University of Miami.

I chose boarding school through my graduation. Evil One didn't know about the boulder in the dandelion field. You see, we really were planning out our future in between kisses. We had decided that Ernesto would attend Yale to be close by until I graduated. His cousin had done the same thing for his girlfriend and subsequently married her when she graduated high school.

I told my mother that I would return to school and stay until grad. (I did not tell her about Ernesto and Yale). Turns out I gave her the wrong answer. I had forgotten that in order to beat my mother you had to take the choice you didn't want and make her think it was the one you wanted with all of your heart.

True to form she took the choice away and told me I would be returning home. No rhyme or reason. That is just a part of who the Evil One was. Remember Hun Academy? What made me happy or content would make her unhappy. She always ruled against me and even went out of her way to sabotage me. I think I was paying for the hatred and the love she felt for my father; and for the part of herself she saw in me.

After the boarding school issue had been settled she sent me to my grandparents to spend the night. My grandmother was out of town and it would be just him and I. Reeling from what had just occurred, the fear of returning to hell overwhelmed me. Something inside of me broke... separated. My grandfather begrudgingly gave me permission to visit some friends in the building. The building was filled with seniors, grand and great-grand parents, mostly Jewish and tons of snowbirds. The grandkids would visit for a week or two and we would all hang out at the pool, by the shuffleboard court, or in the community room.

I met up with my girlfriends in the lobby and we decided to sneak away to a pool at a local hotel called *The Marco Polo*. *The Marco Polo* was three blocks from our building and we weren't supposed to go that far without adult supervision. The girls and I chilled by the pool, flirting with a few boys who were on vacation. As the sun began to lower we were all due back for supper. I made an excuse and didn't go. I ended up with a boy from Brazil, talking and kissing into the night; putting as much emotional distance between myself and my school love as I could. Living for that night the life of some other girl. What I didn't realize then is that I would become that girl for more than three years. As the night wore on we fell asleep on a lounger. I heard voices shouting my name as we ran down the beach. The boy (I cannot remember his name) tried to convince me to go back, but I refused.

As it turns out Brazilian Boy was staying in a different hotel. We spent the day at his pool and the night in his room, careful not to wake his Aunt and Uncle in the adjoining suite. In the morning he introduced me to his aunt and uncle asking if I could stay with him for the rest of their trip. They began asking questions about where my family was. The wanted to speak to my parents, to get permission for me to stay. I told them my family didn't care where I was or what I did. It looked like they were going to allow me to stay. We went with them to dinner that evening (this is now night three since I left, a new record) and they began questioning me again. "How old are you?" "Thirteen." "What's your last name?" Topper (now they had my full name). "Don't your parents miss you?" "NO." I truly believed that no one would miss me. I was inconsequential, if anything I was a burden to those around me.

After dinner we returned to the hotel and I overheard them calling the police.

Sorry, Got To Run!

Upon hearing the call I bolted. As I made my way down the beach I came across a tiki bar and loungers. I made myself at home and stayed close to the people at the bar, for some reason I found comfort in the proximity of others. As the evening wore on I fell asleep on a lounger. In the morning I was starving, broke and bathroom-less. I was afraid to stay on the beach and risk being found and I needed to find a place to get cleaned up. I remembered a county park in North Miami called Greynold's Park, and I headed there. I got myself cleaned up in the public bathroom and settled onto a park bench, making it home for the day.

I was falling asleep as the sun set, when a disheveled rotund black woman came up to me. She reminded me of our Bahamian au pair's mother... Something about her tone was gentle and welcoming. With full knowledge of the answer, Bahama Mama asked me if I had a place to stay. She said this is no place for a "little white girl" and took me to her home, a one room efficiency. It was clean but worn from obvious years of neglect. A low-rent space barely one step up from the projects. I took a shower while she made us supper on her hotplate. There was no couch, only a double bed which we shared for the next couple of days. I remember being so grateful to be where I was. I felt safe.

At some point the next day Bahama Mama told me I had to leave, but could come back in the late evening. She would leave a light on to let me know it was ok to return. As it turns out she was a prostitute. I was so naive I had no idea what that was. I mean really, none. I thought the word "hooking" either meant to steal something or make a shag rug.

I waited from a distance watching men come and go for hours until the porch light was finally turned on and I was able to come back. I only stayed with Bahama Mama for a few days. She told me what she was doing for a living and that she had a drug habit. She urged me to go back home so that I wouldn't end up like her. I told her I would go back home. Bahama Mama will never know this, but in those moments of kindness she saved my life. Not because I returned home, but because of a promise I made to myself as a result of meeting her. I promised myself I would starve before selling my body; and so it was. This woman and these brief moments kept me from selling my body and turning to drugs. This woman who seemingly had nothing to give... fed, sheltered and educated me.

In the days that followed my leaving Bahama Mama I bounced from place to place. For the first several weeks I stood outside of a 7 Eleven gas station, occasionally finding loose change for a pint of milk. Some of the managers would let me straighten up the shelves and such, giving me food in exchange. There were a few regulars who would get their morning coffee or not so afternoon six-pack that would bring out a hot dog or bag of chips for me. As the days passed I got to know a few of them. One guy in particular would hang around a little extra. He was a day laborer that looked like a hippie. He was tall and skinny with long straggly hair that hung to his waist. I can only imagine what I looked and smelled like. I know I no longer had the fat ass my mother accused me of having, not that I ever really did. By now I was skinny... no, I was skeletal. I would wash up in the sink in the 7 Eleven, which is of course a far cry from a shower. I had no change of clothes or toothbrush. I would "brush" my teeth with my finger sans toothpaste and learn how to make tampons from rolled up toilet paper.

One afternoon hippie man invited me for dinner and I of course jumped at the offer. I ended up staying at his house for a few nights, sleeping next to him in a sheer wife-beater he had given me, and my panties. I left after he tried to get me to smoke pot and have sex. I really had no concept that no man takes in a girl without expectation. I went back to the 7 Eleven and would continue sleeping on park benches for many more weeks.

At some point I lucked out and met a really nice kid... He was around 19. He took me in while his parents were in Israel. These were more the kind of people I was used to in terms of background. They were educated, upper middle class Jews. I was at home without the hell.

This boy whose name I cannot remember would end up being my boyfriend for about a month until I had to move on. We played house and did normal "couple" things. Movies, mall, dinner... lazy couch nights. He was also into music and played guitar while I sang poorly. Eventually his parents returned and started asking questions. As the heat became hotter I ran again. I was, however, a little smarter. If these people called the police they would have no accurate information regarding where I came from or what my real name was.

19 MY NEW IDENTITY

For starters I went with 18… which was a stretch as I looked 12. With all the days of not having enough to eat, a month hardly made a dent in putting any significant weight on. I barely looked like I could have reached puberty. My new name? Valentine, pronounced *Valenteen*. She was a character from a Judith Krantz novel that I had just read; Valentine was a Parisian clothing designer in Beverly Hills. She was beautiful, glamorous and strong. Everything I wasn't, except for the strong part. As far as a last name… no clue. I cannot remember. I told people that I was from New York, my parents were dead, and I was an only child. No living relatives. It wasn't a stretch since this is how I felt. It was an easy lie to tell. It was an even easier lie to live.

20 MY RUNAWAY FAMILY.

This is the part of the journey where chronology and haze is really setting in. I am struggling with the time frame. I am not struggling with the events... for the most part. Somewhere between finally finding gainful employment and leaving Florida I met another runaway. We adopted one another as cousins almost immediately. Her name was Lawrie Taveinni (her actual spelling) and she had been on the streets much longer than I. Her story to me was that her father had been a big time cocaine dealer and because he was in jail she had no home. Truth? I will never know. It was certainly possible. These were the years of the cocaine cowboys. We're talking Pablo Escobar and the like. I am getting chills re-entering this phase of my runaway life. Chills and short of breath, I feel like someone is standing on my chest. I have not been back here for a very long time... I have not been back here for over 35 years.

I don't know how much longer Lawrie had been on the streets, or even what her real age was. I do know she had much more knowledge than I. She also had more damage. She could do things I could not. Things like stealing and having sex with pretty much anybody if it meant a roof and food. I would soon learn how to steal like her and avoid the latter.

Lawrie showed me the ropes. She took me from park bench to apartment complex sauna. She always managed fresh clothing, a little cash and tons of make-up. Lawrie wore more make-up than anyone I had ever met. That stands true to this day. Think Tammy Fay eyelashes meets mime. If you aren't familiar with Tammy Fay imagine having a tarantula on each of your eyelids. If you're not familiar with what a mime looks like... white pancake face with bright red lips and cheeks. Lawrie would keep a knapsack stashed in the darnedest of places. In between finding better accommodations we would sleep in the sauna of an apartment complex. Lawrie found a small square panel that was just big enough to tuck her stuff into. She also taught me to steal clothes and the essentials. If I was too freaked out to participate she would do it for me. She was more my older sister than cousin, teaching me everything she knew. I mastered layering new clothes beneath my own while in a dressing room, or if that wasn't an option I would remove the tags and swap the new clothes for the outfit that I wore into the store. I never grew big enough balls to place items in my purse in the middle of the store. Clearly this was before the days of electronic monitoring and ink filled clothing tags.

Lawrie was not into anesthetizing herself, but she did do cocaine on occasion. She drank very little, and most times had her wits about her. We were regulars at a disco called Manhattan's in South Miami. Lawrie knew every drug dealer and their back story. She knew who was the real deal, and more importantly, who to stay away from. It was her relationship with the bouncers that at the age of thirteen and fourteen got us into the club sans identification.

She taught me how to handle cocaine in terms of cutting it into lines to prepare it for use. This "skill" saved me from being kicked out of private parties. Coke-heads tend to be paranoid and if you don't snort, you better act like you do. There were a couple of times I put it on my teeth for show... barely a dab. The cocaine era provided a soft bed without strings for the most part. Men on Coke don't tend to be able to achieve let alone maintain erections. They also don't tend to sleep, which was great since it meant not having to share a bed. If sex did become an issue Lawrie was the one to bed a guy, and seemed to have no issue with it. More times than not it was she who was invited to the parties, and I was the tag-along.

There were times that I was intimate with someone during the Lawrie era, but it would be because I liked the guy and wanted to be his girl. Perpetually looking for love, that was me in a nutshell.

Lawrie always managed to hook us up with food and shelter one way or another. I remember she got us a live-in gig in exchange for "cleaning" some old man's house. By old I mean at least 65 (keep in mind I was thirteenish years old), grey hair, saggy body and super wrinkled. How do I know about his saggy body? He was a nudist... well a perv hiding behind being a nudist. He had a huge, beautiful home; we each had our own rooms complete with en-suite bathrooms. He took us shopping and in the beginning treated us like princesses. Unfortunately, Lawrie neglected to mention the other part of our job description. He wanted us to wear lingerie while one of us jerked him off and the other one rubbed baby powder all over his body. I am cringing as I write this; it's as gross to me now as it was when I almost lived it. Lawrie tried to convince me to do the baby powder and I refused. Then she tried to convince him to just have her, which he did for a few days. Ultimately he ended up kicking us out. She wasn't thrilled with me but at the end of the day I just couldn't do it. We went from his house to breaking into what was supposedly the old house that she shared with her father.

The house was just off of South Dixie Highway, not too far from the old man's house. It had been seized by the Drug Enforcement Administration, and we had to climb over a huge gate in the middle of the night to get into the grounds. It was huge! In fact it wasn't a house, it was a mansion. Everything was marble and the moldings were encrusted in gold leaf, like something out of the movie *Scarface*. There was very little furniture and I only remember a huge oversized king bed which we used until it became unbearable to stay there. Having no running water or electricity made this a very short term solution. After a few days we caved and went back to the sauna.

As the weeks went by, Lawrie, true to form, found better accommodations. She managed to get us into an apartment. We ended up in one room as roommates to a woman and her young daughter. Somehow she pulled some money together to pay rent so the room was really ours instead of some place we were squatting. I got a job as a cashier at a restaurant owned by a retired jockey turned drug dealer called *Neon Leon's*. I liked everything about working there except for the couple who kept on trying to get me to work for them as an escort. The package they offered was pretty attractive and difficult to turn down. If I had been in my earlier days of the run I would have most definitely been sucked in. Who wouldn't want to be paid to simply keep men company and go out to dinner? Lucky for me by this time I knew what a hooker was and that no man paid for simply having dinner. Still they were after me hardcore and it was uncomfortable. They were close friends with the owner and I feared for my job if I offended them. While I was working at Neon Leon's I can remember Lawrie having money, but no job. I never questioned it. Looking back she knew these people and I am pretty sure she was working for them. She would often hang at the bar with them while waiting for me to finish work.

Unfortunately, my new job was very short lived, as was the owner. A few hours after my last shift the owner was shot execution-style by a guy dressed in black on a motorcycle in the parking lot. I wasn't surprised. It was common knowledge that he was a cocaine dealer. Live by the sword, die by the sword... or gun.

Like my job, this apartment of ours also turned out to be short-term. Two girls who had no clue how to be financially responsible were not going to be able to maintain housing for long. Add to the fact that I was making minimum wage at best. At any rate, it was less safe than the sauna. There were more than a few times that men in the area attempted to break in. Miami was overflowing with Mariel boat-lift* criminals and many of them took up space in our neighborhood.

One afternoon as I was ironing my clothes a man broke into the apartment through our patio's sliding glass door. I moved to get away from him and the hot iron landed on my thigh. For years to come you could see a faint outline of the iron on my leg, steam holes and all. Before he was able to get ahold of me I picked up the iron and threatened to burn him with it while screaming for help. I wasn't so silent anymore. The frozen compliant girl had died somewhere between hippie man and Miami Beach. A neighbour rescued me and he took off. The woman we rented from wasn't in any shape to take care of two teens, she could barely provide for her little toddler. Without any money to pay rent we lost the place shortly after that incident. Lawrie being Lawrie never left empty handed. She stole the ladies 35 Beretta. I didn't know it at the time but that bullet-less gun would save me shortly thereafter.

Back in the sauna, unemployed and broke we took to stealing food from the local drug store. I think it was called Eckerd's which is basically a Walgreens or CVS; not a great selection I might add, and it's not like we had a fridge or stove. We lived off of Fritos and canned bean dip. It wasn't so bad, but it would be many years before a Frito would pass my lips again, let alone bean dip. On the upside we had each other, a shower, clothing changes and the gun. I kept it, and even though I knew it wasn't loaded, I felt safer. If it had been loaded I doubt I would have known how to use it. If anything, the lack of bullets probably saved us from accidentally shooting one another.

As I was trying to find a job I would either walk or hitch a ride to an interview or to fill out an application. One would think I would have learned after ending up in a car and being raped, but I didn't. I had nothing to lose anyway. No job equaled no money and no food; no way out. I got into a car with a guy who attempted to put his hands on me shortly into the ride. He grabbed my hand and tried to put it on his penis. You should have seen his face when I pulled the Beretta out! He pulled over immediately, apologizing and begging me not to shoot. This guy turned from animal to weeping baby, he literally had tears in his eyes. Lawrie and I would laugh about that for many days after. The victims were victims no more. The empty gun was our equalizer. I think that's why we found it so funny.

*The Mariel boat-lift was meant to be a vehicle to allow the good citizens of Cuba who wanted to escape the communist regime to immigrate to the United States and begin a new life. The only prisoners that were to be let out were supposed to be political ones. However, the country's dictator, Fidel Castro, had a different plan in mind. He used this opportunity to empty his jails and mental institutions. When the refugee barges docked there was no way to tell the good from the bad.

21 BREAKING & ENTERING…THE FIRST ARREST

Lawrie and I met a couple of guys who owned a house in South Miami where we ended up crashing for about a week. The guys spent their time getting high. They were between construction jobs and didn't seem to care when the next job came up. They literally just hung out all day and night snorting coke. As someone who didn't do cocaine the down side was that users are pretty much never hungry. We would manage to scrape enough together to order pizza or get them to buy food here and there. No matter, clearly a house was better than the sauna. One day, out of the blue, they went off to find work and didn't come back.

We were curious as to where they were but not really fussed, we loved having the house to ourselves. A few days later Lawrie and I were awakened by pounding at the front door. The pounding was sudden and loud, initially it sounded like bombs going off! As we got up we saw armed men through the sheer curtains on the back porch. Given the goings on around us at the time we thought they were hit-men. Turns out it was a S.W.A.T. (Special Weapons and Tactics) team! No joke. Imagine their surprise as they found no cocaine, no drug dealers, and no arms, just two teenage girls shaking like leaves. Actually, I was the only one shaking. Lawrie was the brave no reaction girl. She took it all in stride, just another day. They were so nice as they arrested us for breaking and entering. You could see they felt bad for us. Clearly we were not what they were hoping to find. They could have displayed frustration and even anger that they weren't going to bring in the bad guys. Instead they showed compassion; but nice to us or not, we were in survival mode. We tried to lie and say it was our uncle's house and gave the guys names that had been there. Unfortunately for us it turns out they didn't own the house.

Handcuffed in the back of a police car we stuck to our names, but gave our real age; well Lawrie gave our real age. Being that this was not her first rodeo she knew that lying about our ages would put us in adult jail. We were taken directly to juvenile hall. Here I was, a prep-school kid from a pretty sheltered environment being stripped searched, given granny panties, white keds and scrub-like clothes to wear. I was locked in a cell with a stainless steel toilet and no Lawrie in site. For whatever reason I knew not to cry... Something told me any emotional reaction would result in having the shit kicked out of me. I think I was there for about a week. Funny enough I started to like the place. I attended school, read books, had three meals a day, and the bed was better than a sauna. The down side? The girls did not take to me. I tried to be quiet and invisible, but most of the girls in this place were tough and had been in and out of facilities like this frequently.

Luckily, as things were heating up I was brought to court. My fake name saved me from discovery. No report of me could be found and with no internet or milk cartons with missing children images on them there was nothing to track me back to. I was just another unidentifiable runaway. The judge decided I would best served in a group home.

Happily back in my street clothes, I was driven to a group home which was located in downtown Miami near a bridge. Very nondescript, clean and filled with lots of toys and books. Best part of all there were normal bathrooms and no locked doors on our rooms. There were a handful of kids living there and the counselor on duty was a muscular, middle-aged black man. He looked like an ex-football player, kind of a gentle giant. I liked him instantly. The day I arrived we all went on a field-trip to a park. We played games, and I was pretty happy to be there – with no thought of leaving. This was a huge upgrade from Juvenile hall, let alone the sauna. The counsellor talked to me, but didn't pry or ask too many questions. He was just nice. As we went off to bed he came to my top bunk, "You are safe here, I hope you stay. I am here if you need anything or if you just want to talk." I can still hear his voice, soft and strong at the same time. There was something comforting about him, I felt safe. As I began to doze I heard my name in whispers. It was Lawrie. I don't know how she found me, but she was with a guy who was waiting in a car. I didn't want to leave, but she was the only family I had. I couldn't stay. I couldn't abandon her. As I crept out and ran to the car I could hear the counsellor shouting after me. Off I ran not daring to look back out of the fear that I would see disappointment in his kind face.

Home Sweet Sauna

Back to the sauna. Makes me laugh that the sauna was home. Sauna by night and pool by day a lot of the time; or Manhattan's night club and days of partying on end. That was the majority of my life. All of it was designed to find food and shelter. We were in and out of so many people's houses and apartments it is an absolute blur.

22 A BLURR OF MEMORIES

I remember a guy who looked like Tom Selleck. He was beautiful. Tall and muscular with dark hair, blue eyes and dimples. When I first met him I had the biggest crush on him... I was giddy. I would see him from time to time, but he would avoid any meaningful contact. Clearly he could see I was a child. He used to ask how old I was, knowing I was lying. We would stay at his apartment from time to time and he would cook for us. The last time I saw him he was free basing coke and laying on his back in a stupor on his floor. He was emaciated and had a small pot of water in his hand. There was an egg in the pot... I have no idea if it was ever cooked or eaten. I imagine he didn't survive long given his condition. Such a sad waste of a man, of a life.

Lawrie and I also spent a fair amount of time in the dorms at the University of Miami with college boys. Bouncing back and forth between Pearson and Mahoney Hall. I think we would meet these kids at Manhattan's and they would invite us back to their rooms. We never stayed long; there was no way to set up house in a one room flat with dorm monitors and roommates. It was fun though, we pretended for a moment that we too were carefree college students.

In addition to Manhattan's we would do the cocaine night club circuit in Coconut Grove. Faces was a pretty popular hangout, as was Monty's restaurant. We ended up living in some guys penthouse in Grove Isle for a few weeks before he went to jail for dealing. Lawrie, fast on her feet as she was, stole his credit card on our way out. We ended up staying at the Mutiny hotel enjoying room service and shopping for a week. The spree ended when the card maxed out.

There was one time I thought I was busted. I ran into my brother Steven's step-mother in line while buying a pair of jeans. I saw her before she saw me and turned my back quickly in hopes to pay and leave undiscovered. Before I got to the register she "made" me. She asked if I had spoken to my mother. I lied and said yes, of course. She kept asking what I had been up to, trying to make small talk. Before another word could fall from her mouth I abruptly said "bye" and ran out of the store. There wasn't really anything that she could have done; this was a time before main stream cell phone ownership and there was no such thing as the internet, let alone email. She had no way of knowing whether I was still missing. She wasn't close to anyone in my family.

She did speak with Steven and learned the truth, but it was much too late. I was gone. I think this was only a few months into my run, but I can't know for sure. It is just one of many blurred memories.

23 I WAS A DRUG DEALER'S GIRLFRIEND

I can't remember his name in real life but they called him Flaco, which is Spanish for skinny, and he was. I don't remember him doing drugs, I think he was just built lean. I liked him, he was strong and good looking. I felt protected and special to be "his" girl. Lucky for me it didn't last long. We were in the early stages of dating and had not yet become physical, but as far as he was concerned I was his property. It came to an early end when he saw a guy talking to me and lost his shit. I thought he was going to gun him down and at a minimum hit me. That was the end of that almost relationship. I have to say that it was fun for a blip. Fast car, first class service and fancy restaurants. In contrast to the sauna, Motel 6 looked good. I thought I had hit it big and I really thought that I liked him. Rumour has it he could get extremely violent with those that crossed him. He always had weapons and a very short fuse for sure. Clearly I dodged a bullet or two... literally.

I dodged a lot of bullets. I always managed to land on my feet; and I still do. In those times, as long as I had Lawrie, I had somewhere I belonged. Occasionally we would get separated for short periods of time, but we had made a pact that should we become separated we would meet back at the sauna, no matter what. Keep in mind there were few cell phones back then… (not that we could have afforded one, let alone two) and they were prohibitively expensive. In fact they were mostly in the possession of drug dealers and a few wealthy businessmen. Both of my Daddies' owned cell phones that came with big boxes that had shoulder straps to make them "portable."

I hated when I ended up sleeping in the sauna alone. It was terrifying. We wouldn't go into them until after 9 or 10 at night to be sure no one was using them. Sometimes I could hear people coming and I was afraid they would kick me out, leaving me unable to find Lawrie. I remember one night that was particularly cold. Our bag that was hidden in the paneling was missing and I had nothing soft to put my head on. No clothes to cover me for warmth other than what I had on. I attempted to work the sauna for heat but I didn't know how. So I lay there alone on the wooden slats, shivering in the dark... weeping. At first I began to cry for my Mother. True story, I began to cry for the Evil One. I wanted her to rescue me... I wanted her to love me. I wondered out loud if she even remembered who I was. Slowly I came to my senses and began whispering to my Daddy in heaven to please help me. I believed he was the only one who could and the only one who would care. A dead man, nothing left but soul and ashes. Thoughts of my Daddy soothed me, focused me. I decided that I was going through this hell as a kind of pre-payment for a good life. From a very young age I always knew that better days lay ahead. Now I had an explanation as to why. I was paying up front. I decided that I was destined for greatness and I just had to power through.

That same night I was discovered and kicked out. More than discovered. One of the maintenance men tried to rape me. I managed to fight him off and I ran. I lost Lawrie for a few days, but stayed in the area. I don't remember where I slept in the days after the sauna until I found her. In fact I don't remember much of anything from those few days.

24 THE FOSTER HOME

Now we had no changes of clothes, food or money. Tired of Eckerd's Fritos and bean dip we set out for the mall. We stole clothes from Jordan Marsh to change into and went into a grocery store located in the same mall. Unfortunately, we didn't notice the undercover security guard following us from the department store.

We ate our way up and down the aisles opening up cookies and such all the while tucking food in our clothes and purses. As we exited the store, mall security was laying in wait. Arrested again. I wasn't so upset or scared this time. I figured it would either be juvenile hall or the group home. I liked the thought of the group home and had decided this time I would stay there. Maybe they would even send Lawrie there with me.

I spent a couple of weeks in Juvenile Hall before a judge sent me to a foster home. The foster mother was a rotund black woman who was far from warm and welcoming. Looking back it's clear that we were her income, and there were quite a few of us, ranging in age from four to sixteen years old. The house was immaculate thanks to all of the free slave labor. When I arrived, there were children doing dishes, vacuuming and dusting while the foster mom sat eating in front of the television. One of the kids filled me in on how the house was to be cleaned every day, and that I should expect to be doing a ton of laundry. She took me on a tour and then brought me to my new room. I was going to be sharing a room with two girls that were sisters. As she began to introduce me I recognized the girls as kids I went to elementary school with. The younger one was the same age as I, and we were friends in school. Her sister was three years older and a very tough cookie. It turns out the younger sister had become tough like her big sis. Before I could offer my friendship they told me to take off or they were going to kill me. I believed them. These were not kids from my original neighbourhood. We never crossed paths outside of school. These were hardened girls. I drew on my memory of the older sister beating a boy to a bloody pulp. She was in grade six at the time and her sister and I were third graders. He was massive compared to her and she had him on the ground in a ball. He was crying and begging her to stop. With this scene in mind I didn't take more than a moment. I grabbed my bag and was ready to go. As I tried to make my way to the door they cornered me in the bedroom next to an open window. They pulled my knapsack out of my hands and pushed me backwards against the wall. I leapt out the window running as fast as my legs would carry me.

As I ran down the sidewalk I realized I had no Lawrie and no idea where I was. I also had no money, no food and no clothes. Back to square one... well, almost. At least now I had some more survival skills to draw on which I would use until I found Lawrie or she found me.

25 LIFE AFTER LAWRIE

I somehow made my way down to South Miami Beach. Sounds glamorous, doesn't it? Well it wasn't. South Beach was nothing like what most know it to be now. Back then it was the early eighties and several of the old art deco hotels were getting a much needed facelift, it was the beginning of the redevelopment of the area. Other than that nothing good was happening down there. The Mariel boat-lift was in full swing and I was in the middle of it.

In the beginning of the boat-lift I would sit on the rocks near South Pointe Pier and watch the barges filled with refugees, political and violent criminals coming in. As the Mariels kept coming with no end in sight, the streets were becoming increasingly unsafe to walk; girls were literally being raped in broad daylight in the streets. Violent crime was so prevalent and out of control that the *Guardian Angels came in from New York to police the streets. The Angels had the full support of the local authorities who could not handle this influx of crime.

The area was riddled with abandoned art deco buildings and cocaine dealers. It was an ongoing scene from *Scarface*, guns blazing and all.

Most of the nightclubs during this time were decorated with mirrored tables, not for aesthetics, but for function. People were snorting cocaine off of these tables right out in the open. The conversations in the ladies bathrooms circled around which men had the most coke and who would be the most generous with it.

I may have been a stranger to prostitution, but the same could not be said of drugs. Between my Manhattan Club night's education and Lawrie, cocaine was no longer a new drug to me. As for other drugs like quaaludes and speed, I recognized them well from my childhood. I knew what it meant to be into drugs and I knew what drugs turned you into.

*The Guardian Angels is an international volunteer organization of unarmed crime-prevention patrollers.

My mother and brother were in a constant battle over drugs. Not the kind of battles you would think, not the way it should have been. She wasn't hounding him to stop doing drugs. She was after him for stealing hers, and often times they would put me in the middle. In fact my mother and brother were constantly stealing drugs from one another. He would ask me if I saw her go into his closet or his stash. She would ask me if I saw him taking anything from her room. I always said no to her, and when my brother asked I told him the truth. I had his back... or so I thought. She of course would tell him that I told her I saw him in her room stealing her pills. My Mother's behaviour resulted in him hating me for extended periods of time. He never believed me when I told him that I had said nothing. As my big brother he otherwise loved me, but as her son he resented me. She did this by design. Divide and conquer. To this day my brother and I have no relationship. He no longer does drugs and hasn't since he left her "supervision." He made it out, but his need for her love and approval keeps him tied tightly to her apron strings.

Back to the Evil One's drug use. Her drugs of choice were marijuana, hashish, black beauties (amphetamines) and quaaludes for the most part. She kept her pot in the freezer and had a crystal ashtray in her bedroom filled with an assortment of pills. Being around drugs had no effect on me... There was no temptation or curiosity. I had not only decided I would never do them because of her but because of Bahama Mama as well. I had also realized early on that E.O's lack of control was directly related to her drug use. I had no desire to be out of control – and now my survival depended on it.

After a couple of weeks I had let go of the thought that I would find Lawrie. I knew I needed to fend for myself, and focus on my survival. I began hanging around a pizza joint on Lincoln Road called Big Daddy's. Finding loose change here and there I would buy a slice or the like, and the manager at the 7 Eleven would feed me in exchange for busing tables. Big Daddy's by day and abandoned buildings by night.

I was fourteen brushing fifteen years old, a waif of a person sleeping in condemned and abandoned buildings with cock roaches and rats as my roommates. I would sleep upright against a wall on the concrete floor. I always stayed near stairs or a doorway to be ready to run if I needed to. This was definitely the lowest point of my life on the streets. I would sometimes bathe fully clothed in the ocean as my options were few. Occasionally I would manage to use a shower in one of the hotels if I could sneak in. I can recall one time I had the stomach flu and no bathroom. I had shit all over my pants. It was horrible and embarrassing. I had to wait until it was dark to make my way to the ocean to clean myself up. Even though I would often be dirty I would make every effort to find my way clean. I had a sense of pride and these moments were unbearable. I find it hard to write these things. I am profoundly embarrassed about these moments to this day.

Somehow my luck eventually turned for the better. I had managed to steal a new outfit and had clean clothes for a change. I can picture the outfit in vivid detail. Nothing fancy, just fun and trendy for the time. It was a pair of turquoise skinny jeans and a silky cream colored blouse with a brightly coloured lion that looked to have been hand-painted with watercolours.

Maybe it was the outfit that turned my luck. I was walking through an art show in my new threads on the streets of South Beach; as I was admiring the scenery, a handsome man in his thirties began talking to me. He turned out to be a very successful businessman. He made his living flipping huge houses before flipping became a thing. These were not just any houses. These were beautiful old waterfront homes in Miami Beach, most had at least five bedrooms and beautiful old moldings to work with. There was something about him that I trusted and I liked right away. Maybe it was the fact that he took me in and fed me... like a stray puppy.

I can't remember the sequence of events, but I ended up staying with him for several weeks. As I was settling in as his girlfriend he was not just taking care of me. He was also trying to help me get a job so that I could be independent. Just one problem. As I was applying for jobs in big hotels on the beach they all required identification prior to hiring me. I couldn't tell him that I had no identification. He would have insisted we go to the Department of Motor Vehicles to obtain ID and well, it's not like I really existed. The result of my not getting a job was him thinking that I didn't want to work. As he put the pressure on I did what I do best, I ran. He was very difficult to leave. I felt safe with him, but I knew I couldn't tell him the truth. Ironically, sadly and happily I found a job a few days after I ran. I should have gone back to him, but I didn't know how to. I was sure he had forgotten me and if he hadn't I was sure he wouldn't forgive me.

I began working at Lums, an American style diner, as a waitress. It was on Collins Avenue near one of the condos that I lived in when my daddy was alive. I knew the area really well and I liked being near the old building. Unfortunately I only lasted three days at Lums... Apparently food service wasn't for me. I got fired for bitching at the manager. To be fair he was in the kitchen behind a partition and I thought I was telling the cook off. He kept messing up my orders and it was making the lunch rush a nightmare. The final straw came when a customer threatened not to tip because of his screw-up. I decided my best bet after that would be to try to find a job as a cocktail server. More money, shorter shifts, and no cooks.

My first pick was the Fontainebleau Hotel. Even though I had no identification I thought it was worth a shot. I loved that place, it was gorgeous! I figured I could serve in the pool area and get a tan while I worked. In my quest to find a job there I met some of the valet guys and became friends with one whom I had recognized from living in abandoned buildings. He told me he found an efficiency in the Lorraine Hotel on Collins Avenue, and if I needed a place to crash I was welcome. He did not become a romance, just my bedmate without benefits. That's what fellow runaways do. We become one another's family. We do our best to try to help one another to fight our way out of homelessness.

As with many of the people that I came to know during my life on the streets I cannot remember his name. It doesn't bother me so much when it is a roommate kind of person but it really bothers me that I cannot remember the name of the guy who flipped houses. We were boyfriend/girlfriend and I cannot pull his name up. I find it really disturbing, shameful even.

I'm going to call Fontainebleau guy Runner-boy, since that's what he was. Runner-boy wasn't getting enough shifts at the Fontainebleau and he was on the hunt to find a second job. He had heard of a job at a family owned pub and because they were opening additional bars he thought I might be able to find something as well, so I tagged along. This marks the period of my finally becoming gainfully and consistently employed. The family, known as the Flynn's, were opening a disco and hired me as a cocktail waitress, no questions asked. It turned out to be a pretty cool spot in the Seville Hotel on Collins Avenue. To top it off it was a short walk from our efficiency. I loved my new job, easy money, easy work and no pressure.

I was rapidly saving money to move out on my own, life was amazing... not just good. It took me just over a month to pull together enough cash for first and last, plus some. Here I was fourteen and about to have my own place. It's pretty crazy to look back and realize how young I was. I excitedly began apartment hunting and was looking forward to having my very first apartment. I found a little place that was still within walking distance to work and made my way back to the efficiency to get cash for the deposit and sign my lease. I didn't have a bank account, no identification = no account. I kept my money in a drawer with my clothes and other personal items. You can see what's coming next, can't you? I didn't. No money. I mean none. I had saved eleven hundred dollars and it was gone. Runner-boy had justified taking it because I hadn't been paying rent. Rent that he told me I didn't have to pay since I was buying us food. Even if I was to pay rent it would have been a quarter of what I had saved. I stayed a few more days and used my tips to move into my own efficiency.

Fortunately tips at the disco were plentiful. The place being new stayed pretty busy with locals, and had a consistent flow of tourists that were staying at the hotel. I also had a very generous regular. He used to come in a couple of times a week and tip me a fifty or one hundred dollar bill for one or two drinks. Eventually he began hanging out more and more, talking to me, more and more. I didn't like him, he was old and greasy, but I did like the high dollar tips. Naturally that was my focus. As a result of the big tipper I was way ahead of the game and able to stay in the black. I still couldn't get a real apartment because I couldn't save enough money for first and last while also paying for an efficiency. I wanted a cheaper place, but I was happy to have my own roof regardless. Life was good. Not bad for a kid who had never held a real job or had any clue of how to pay a bill.

26 A PROMISE TESTED

Unbeknownst to me my big tipper nights were about to come to an end. Mr. Big Tipper came in as usual, but instead of his regular table he sat at the bar. My shift was over and I was helping to clean off the bar making small talk with the bartender. Out of the blue Mr. Big Tipper took out five thousand dollars and slapped it down in front of me and the bartender. "This is yours if you have sex with me one time." This is literally what he said. I have to tell you that I looked at that money for a long time. My first thoughts were about how life changing it would be for me. This was the early eighties; five thousand dollars could purchase a brand new car. Five thousand dollars could pay rent for well over a year. As I said, life changing. I just stood there, mouth open, wide eyed... focusing on what five thousand dollars would buy: security. And then I looked at him. A big bearded Mulatto man at least fifty pounds overweight, probably in his fifties and... just gross looking overall. On top of that I could not tell you one interesting thing about him. In all of the times I had served and spoken to him, he made no impression on me. He had no redeeming quality unless you call money a quality. I was a child and he was nothing more than a dirty old man. I thought about my promise next. I thought about the other part of life changing that taking this money for sex would represent. How it would redefine me and make my mother right, how it would make me just like my mother. I would officially become a tramp. I declined, and that was the last I ever saw of him. The male bartender was like "Hell, I would have slept with him for half that'! We had a good laugh and I went home with no regrets.

As my big tipper was gone and on normal days tips were up and down, my efficiency living was proving to be less than efficient, financially speaking. I was beginning to have a hard time maintaining and needed to move somewhere that was more affordable. There was a horrible building on the brink of being condemned in one of the prettiest areas of the beach. It was on Biscayne and Collins across from the then demolished dog track. There were no high rises and my flat had an unobstructed view of the ocean, and of the Mariels being barged in. I was in the hood. There was a row of honky-tonk bars and an abundance of guys with prison tats. My building, which has long since been torn down, survived only by Joe's Stone Crab, was infested with cockroaches that more than a few times ran across my back as I slept. Drunks screaming and sounds of domestic violence in the night was commonplace. All that said it was a roof, and unlike abandoned buildings it also had a bed and a door that locked. If memory serves it was around $30.00 per week; I could do a month there for the weekly cost of the efficiency.

Even after lowering the rent, money was tight. I could walk to work during the day, but for safety reasons I had to cab it back at night unless I managed to get a ride. To stretch out meals chicken stew was pretty much what I was living on. I can't remember why that became the meal other than it being cheap and easy to stretch. I lived on it for so long that the thought of any kind of stew causes me to gag to this day. I will definitely never eat anything that resembles chicken stew, never again.

The disco closed and I started working in another of the Flynn's bars, which was called Flynn's. It was a pub atmosphere with live music. Other than living in the hood, life was good and about to get better. I was singing along to the juke box as I began my first shift, and in walked Michael T. I think I froze in my tracks... I know I stopped singing (which was a good thing). I was 15 at this point and even with all the scraped knees I received in the year plus on the road I was still very much a naive little school girl that believed in happy endings and Prince Charming.

Michael was about to be my major crush. He was a muscly 6'5" with long brown curly hair and hazel eyes. He walked... no strode in with his guitar case, southern draaaawlll, and a huge white grin. "Hello Daaarrrlin!" I'm Michael. Aren't you a pretty little thing!" I was done! A country singer from Tampa who turned to music when his baseball career ended almost before it began. He came from a few ball players, his father and brother both played for the reds. FYI; I don't like or care about baseball. It's like watching paint dry. Anyway, not unlike most girls I am a sucker for a tall hot guy who sings and plays the guitar. We became a couple almost instantly. To add to the appeal (not that he needed to) Michael also had a beautiful white Russian husky name Misha. The two of them moved in with me almost immediately and it was bliss.

We would go to work together, sleep late and swim with Misha in the ocean during the day. We even found the sweetest little kitten that would ride on Misha's back as he swam. Cutest thing ever. As the area was beyond dangerous, prior to Michael I would only walk the street when I had to. When he moved in I only left the apartment with him or Misha, per Michael's instructions. He kept me safe. The months were passing uneventfully until Michael's brother Billy and his wife, Janis came to town. They moved down the hall from us and our "perfect" life took a new course. Billy was also a singer/guitar player, he and Michael started performing together at Flynn's. Money was becoming an issue because Michael was paying Billy out of his own pocket.

To top it all off Billy could be a huge handful. Billy, who towered over Michael would drink tequila and climb telephone poles, piss drunk. I'm not even kidding... or exaggerating. His wife was an emaciated looking chain smoker with a wicked bad cough. She waitressed at a diner and fit the part. She is what you would expect to see at a truck stop. Eventually the Flynn's tired of Billy's shenanigans and told Michael he had to go. Michael being a loyal little brother decided to pack it in as well. The boys weren't able to find a replacement gig and decided that Daytona Beach was the land of opportunity. The next week we made the four hour drive to Daytona, also known as the land of the teenage runaways; it would have been a runaway's paradise, but for the pedophiles out-numbering us. Fortunately I had Michael.

27 SINGING POORLY ON DAYTONA NIGHTS

Me, not Michael. Somehow Michael got it in his head that this "cute little gal" could sing. I guess love is deaf. He had me singing in the background and a few songs not so background. I didn't mind singing behind him, actually I loved it. He and Billy found us a gig at a little motel bar right on the beach. The job came with a little money and two efficiencies. Billy's wife worked at the diner and Billy told the owner that I had bartending experience. Fortunately for me I could fake it. It helps that drinks weren't so complicated back then, the 'art of mixology,' wasn't a thing; and most bottles had drink recipes on the labels for things like Grasshoppers and Tom Collins. I tended bar and sang back up. All was good, better than good. The chicken stew days were behind us and we were no longer living in the "hood."

We worked nights, slept late and beached by day. There was no rent to pay and we had a little money in our pockets. Life was stable and simple; and then Billy climbed up a telephone pole. Of course being true to form, Billy had to make it really bad. He chose the pole directly in front of the motel. The owner, a little brown man with a thick Indian accent, was yelling at Billy to get down. The next thing we knew life wasn't so good. The police were called to get Billy off of the pole. It was pretty funny to watch as the police attempted to get this huge man – 6'5 plus, with a beer belly resembling that of a woman carrying twins – off of the pole. How he even had the agility to climb the telephone poll was a feat in and of itself! The next morning after Billy had slept of the tequila he had the pleasure of dealing with wifey, who was less than happy. Looking back, I feel like she was always unhappy. Who could blame her?! Unhappy or not she stood (they are together to this day) by her man like a bad country song. After Billy's less than Cirque Du Soleil performance we were all fired. I went on the hunt for a new job as Michael tried to book a solo gig.

I landed at job as a bartender at the Kings Inn Hotel. Sounds like nothing, but it turned out to be my very good luck. There were nightly shows and the headliner was an ex-actress/burlesque dancer named Babette Bardot. It turns out that she had been the highest paid stripper in the U.S. in the late sixties. She performed regularly at the infamous Pink Pussycat in Los Angeles for $2500.00 per week. Her 44-24-38 frame brought in hoards of men to see her burlesque review. The bar had a cover to weed out the riff-raff and most of the clients were businessmen with money to burn. The tips were great.

Babette was also the hotel owner's girlfriend and everything revolved around her. Even so she behaved like a grounded star. She was sweet and humble with no airs about her. She was the epitome of glamorous and had an accent to boot. I used to run food up to her penthouse: it was like something out of a movie. There she would be with her perfectly coifed platinum blond hair, body draped in a silky penoir with matching furry mules, sprawled on a chaise lounge in all her glory. I wanted to be her...with my clothes on.

Billy was angry at Michael for not wanting to play together. I was angry at Michael for keeping Billy around. Billy's wife hated me for not being a wrinkled haggard shrew. As if that wasn't enough the cocktail waitress, a runaway named Candle (no joke) threatened to kick my arse if I made her tip out. At this point my days of cowering were over. Well, they were over until she tried to double team me with her sister Wick... Ok not Wick, Amber. Same difference. I ran down the beach with them chasing me back to our motel. That was the last straw for all of us. Michael decided it was time to go back to his hometown: Tampa.

We arrived at Michael's mom's house in the wee hours of the morning. She was sleeping and as we were exhausted we went to bed straight away. Billy and wifey took the truck (pickup of course, we are in the country music world after all) and checked into a motel. We were in the middle of suburbia, a modest house that was definitely a home. The decor was warm and woodsy. Michael's mom... I think her name was Barbara, spoke with a country drawl. She was all southern hospitality. She was a slightly round woman who stood about my height (5'3) with short black hair in that typical old fifties kind of hair-sprayed style. I took to her immediately and her to me. I didn't know it at the time, but moving in with Barbara would mark the end of mine and Michael's relationship.

Our accommodations changed dramatically. Barbara was having none of our sleeping in the same room arrangement. I think she knew how young I was and took me into her "protection." I didn't need or want that sort of protection. At this point I had been living life as an adult too long to be treated like a child. All I needed was Michael. I thought I loved him and was terrified of not being with him. Looking back at this point in my life I thought that my sexuality was what kept a man. I thought if we weren't having sex he would go elsewhere. I wasn't wrong about the last part. For so many months he had been my solid ground. We weren't sleeping together anymore and only stealing intimate moments here and there; Michael began going out without me. He would be gone for a couple of days at a time with little to no explanation. I might have been young but I certainly wasn't stupid. I came to learn that he was hooking up with his ex-girlfriend who also happened to be his first love. She was a force to be reckoned with. She was an ex-ballet dancer and had the body to prove it, she was an adult AND she and Michael had history. I was losing him at warp speed and helpless to do anything about it.

28 RUN, RUNAWAY, RUN

Unhappy, I did what came naturally. I began to plan my exit. As a runaway staying put and addressing problems head-on is not an option. At this stage of my life I wasn't running out of fear, I was running because it was just the only way I knew to deal with unhappiness. Runaways do not face problems no matter the size. We just leave and put them seemingly behind us. That is how we control our environment and manage out pain... or deflect from our pain. We create a new anxiety to focus on, we move, we look for a new job... We do whatever we have to do to not feel pain or rejection.

As Michael was around less and less, I no longer felt at home. I never felt as if I really had the right to stay in his house, but as his girlfriend I at least felt like I somehow belonged. Without him I had no relationship to tie me to the house. Looking back I realize that his mom loved me. I am sure she never knew that I only felt I had a place there because of Michael. Thanks to Evil One I never felt valued by anyone and I always reacted from that head and heart space. Without a doubt I could have stayed there indefinitely. Regardless, I found a job fairly quickly and moved into a motel room.

My first job in Tampa Bay was as a bartender at a huge country music club. The manager hired me with the understanding that I would produce identification within the week. Without a doubt he knew I was not of age and unbeknownst to me he had a solution in mind. Still, I hoped I could get it past him. The club was so busy that I thought there was a good chance that he wouldn't remember to follow-up. I was wrong. No matter what was going on he was never too busy to follow up. He asked me for my ID everyday for almost two weeks. I can't remember what excuses I gave, but I thought he would eventually give up if I worked extra hard and proved my value. I wanted – no, *needed* – to keep my job. I was already happy there, making new friends and great money. At the rate I was going I was going to be able to get a real place to live in no time.

One night as we were cleaning the bar, my boss told me to wait in his office. As I sat there waiting I didn't realize that all of the other employees had left. He came in, shut the door and plopped down on his big leather chair. As he sat there, never once taking his eyes off of me, he leaned back and clasped his hands across his big beer gut. He stared at me for what seemed an eternity before he finally spoke. I thought I was about to be fired. "Girl, you and I both know you ain't of age to work here. Lucky for you, I'm a nice guy and I don't want you to be out of a job." As I breathed a sigh of relief he continued on. "I'm thinking I can keep you on if you're willing to do me a favour or two." I sat there wide-eyed thinking I would have to work doubles, or take a cut in pay... Or something of that sort. I didn't see what was coming next. "My wife, she's not taking care of business and a man has needs.

Maybe you could give me a B.J. here and there and we'll call it even. You do that and I will overlook the identification thing." I leapt to my feet as fast as I could and ran out of the office. I didn't even return for my pay-check, I was too scared and embarrassed. A few days later I found a job as a cocktail server in a run-down honky-tonk making far less money.

I managed to find a motel room close to the honky-tonk and lived off of the $1.29 Dunkin' Donuts soup of the day – EVERY day. As the weeks passed and customers became my regulars I was promoted to barmaid. Michael was coming around to my new digs and quickly losing his lustre. I was hurt and felt used. He was no longer my partner in crime. Now he was just an occasional guest that rarely stayed the night. Again I was young, but not stupid.

One of my regulars at the bar took a "special" liking to me. He began tipping extra well and bringing me small gifts. He was a middle aged man with a good job... Compared to me anyway. I looked at him in a parental way clueless to him looking at me as anything but his child; given that I was only fifteen this was my natural conclusion. He was of average height with a bit of a belly. He was not ugly, but also not handsome. He had caramel coloured hair with light eyes and a full beard. I can picture him, but have no recollection of his name. I do however remember him teaching me the term "Mons Pubis." No, I did not show him mine. He would tell me in great detail how he thought that was the most beautiful part of a woman's body. Disappointed, I quickly began to realize he was not looking at me like a daughter. As he turned up the heat I knew a proposition was only a matter of time. I began job hunting right away hoping to find something before the heat became a raging fire.

As I was responding to want ads Michael kept turning up like a bad penny. I decided it was over and wouldn't open the door to him anymore. I finally found a job as a traveling salesperson for a "miracle" all-in-one cleaning product. I still had a few things left at Barbara's house and went to retrieve them. I excitedly filled her in on my new job. I was looking forward to the travel and the money that I would be making. I told her that our first major stop was going to be in West Virginia and that we would be training along the way. She wasn't impressed. She asked me to move back in and get a regular job, or go to school. She said I could stay as long as I wanted.

Michael came home in the midst of things and begged me to stay swearing he would change. When this girl gets hurt there is no going back. I told them I would stay in touch and off I went without looking back.

29 CAN I INTEREST YOU IN "AMAZING 901?"

The next day a van came to pick me up. There were four kids my age, three girls and one boy already in the van. Our bosses were a couple of low-brow middle aged men. We hit the road, all of us kids were giddy with excitement. We were looking forward to traveling all over the U.S. and making tonnnnnssss of commission. All of our expenses, hotel and food would be covered. No more Dunkin' Donuts soup; I had hit the big-time!

The product we were selling was called "Amazing 901." It removed ink and grease from fabric plus any other stain or dirt you could dream up. "Amazing 901" was sold in a concentrate and you could buy it by the gallon, dilute it with water and it would last forever... well almost forever. We would go into auto repair shops and dealerships pedalling the product by writing on our jeans, then a little spray and dab and Presto! Stain gone. Of course the bottle of 901 that we used to demo was not so diluted and it worked like gangbusters as a result. When we ran out of car dealers and garages we would hit suburbia and go door to door. We did this from Tampa Bay to Point Pleasant, West Virginia. I cannot remember how much I sold, but it was enough for me to be excited about my first pay check. As payday approached I could sense that things were not going to go smoothly. There was something in the way that our bosses kept making comments about the expenses; they kept going on and on about the cost of the food and motels.

We checked into the Lowes Hotel in Point Pleasant, two to a room. We all felt like something was off. There was just no escaping that uneasy feeling that began to take root. It didn't help that this place had the reputation of being haunted and the interior looked like the hotel in the movie "The Shining." The kitchen could have been the one in the movie, it was eerily similar. Because there was no room service, the hotel allowed the guests access to the kitchen. I remember going there late one night and running out terrified, like a bat out of hell. One little noise and I was off like a shot, better to go to bed hungry than dead.

The four of us went to get our pay and we were each handed thirty dollars. We were not only selling the "Amazing 901," we were also working seven days a week. We were not allowed to take a day off. Thirty dollars. That's all that was left after they deducted our food and lodging. Of course we argued, but it was a losing proposition. We were trapped like indentured servants. Who were we going to tell? Where were we going to go? I figured it was better than nothing and at least I wasn't in a sauna or abandoned building. Clearly, the other kids felt the same way as they stayed put as well.

In the days that followed we traveled to Ohio. The first major stop was Columbus. I was dropped off with my bottle and rag in a student housing area. It didn't take me long to realize that college students were not our demographic. Most were struggling to make ends meet, and cleaning was not high on their priority list. As I knocked on doors I met a girl who was crashing with her college boyfriend. She invited me in and said he would buy, I just had to wait until he got home. She was a pretty petite hippie type with long wavy blonde hair. She made some food and asked me how I ended up selling door to door. It is true what they say about birds of a feather. I knew she was a runner and she had lucked into a good place; she knew I hadn't. As it turned out hippie girl's boyfriend was broke. I was anything but disappointed. Hippie girl made us food and we ate, listened to records and hung out like best friends. The best part was that I got to be a kid for a few hours. On my way out the door hippie girl gave me a big hug and told me I could come back and crash anytime.

As winter began to take hold we left Columbus for other parts of Ohio. Being from Florida none of us had winter boots or warm coats. We would walk door to door in the snow with our samples, praying someone would let us in even if it was only for a moment. Most of the neighbourhoods we were working were pretty rural and the houses were quite far apart. If nobody was home it would be a much longer walk in the cold with no relief from the elements. We were miserable, shivering and frozen to the core. It was so cold on one of the days, that my jaw froze... solid. I literally could not open my mouth to speak when a lady opened her door. Thankfully she invited me in and bought a gallon. After I left her house I began to cry. As my tears froze on my cheeks I knew I needed to find a way out.

30 PLAYING HOUSE

As sales began to dwindle due to frozen children we made our way to a warmer Louisiana. The little bits of money I had earned I saved and used to make my escape in Lake Charles. I went to the mall, threw out my samples and began going from store to store filling out job applications.

I found a job at a women's shoe store, and a room at a nearby motel. As I began to get my bearings I met a girl who worked for Merle Norman. She was a super sweet blond that looked like eating was an option that she chose not to partake in. Think size zero. We bonded immediately over fashion and the like. She invited me out on a blind double date with her boyfriend and his friend. They were a couple of successful yuppie types who worked for Schlumberger, a huge oil and gas company. My guy to be was probably fifteen to twenty years older than I was. He was cute and soft-spoken. I liked him right away. I ended up moving out of my motel room and in with him in record time. The four of us hung out quite a bit. I was really happy to have friends and a place where I felt a sense of belonging. My lifestyle took an upturn. The apartment was in a nice complex, Mr. Schlumberger was educated and from an upper middle class upbringing. This new life was a far cry from the honky-tonk touring days of a country singer's girlfriend. No roach infested rooms, no ex-cons to serve beer to and no Billy shimmying up telephone poles.

I had arrived... or so I thought. The upside to being a runaway is that you never get so comfortable that you can't switch gears. You can go from feast to famine without feeling crushed. We don't expect disappointment, we just handle it well. Runaways live in a partially numb world at all times. That's our armor. Sadly, there is a flip side; we also don't experience deep love or happiness. Numb is numb in all directions.

As with many relationships, initially things were great with Mr. Schlumberger. He was generous and fun to be around. We would go to company functions like Crawfish boils, football games, concerts and big dinners. Every now and again someone would comment or question why he was with such a young girl. The usual questions about my past would surface, but I was well versed on my short, but bittersweet story. I held my own as well as a fifteen year old passing herself off as eighteen could.

As the weeks passed the cracks became apparent. I think Mr. Schlumberger began to realize how immature I was. Even if I had actually been eighteen he was in his thirties. What did he really expect? I still had my job, but I didn't contribute to the household expenses, nor did he expect me too. He did, however, expect I would at least help with the upkeep of the apartment. Which I didn't. It wasn't because I was being lazy, I just didn't think to do it. He had a maid that came in twice a week. It was a two bedroom apartment and it wasn't like there was much to do. Sadly and selfishly, I didn't contribute anything more than my company.

My poor Mr. Schlumberger, he would often go out of town and come back to a bikini clad girl lying by the pool flirting with the neighbors. The much younger, college student neighbors that I, at fifteen, had much more in common with. Not good. I think the straw that broke the camel's back was the time he came home and found me passed out on the sofa with an empty pizza box next to me. I rarely drank and I had gone out with the Merle Norman girl and her boyfriend. Three or four B52 shots, one round of puking and three or four more shots later we made our way home. I don't even remember ordering the pizza. I do remember having bed-spins and eating on the insistence of Merle Norman girl. A few days later Mr. Schlumberger moved me out and into a little studio apartment.

Shortly after moving into my new place I lost my job at the shoe store. The owner's fiancé was not pleased with this pretty little girl spending so much time alone with her guy. Given that we were the only staff in the store it was kind of difficult not to be on our own together. Sad thing was, I didn't do anything wrong nor did he even try to make a move. He was loyal and I had no interest in someone else's man.

Fortunately it was a fairly large mall and I had options. I found another job in the mall's arcade within a few days of being fired. I can probably still fix a pinball machine to this day. Such useful skills I picked up along my journeys.

Lucky for me, Mr. Schlumberger was a prince of a guy to the end. He could have simply kicked me out and I would have deserved it. Being the gentleman that he was he not only arranged for my studio apartment, he also paid a few months rent in advance. To top it off, he had the utilities turned on and scheduled the installation of cable TV.

In the days waiting for the cable technician I had no source of entertainment in my flat. Bored and lonely, I found my way to a nearby Black Angus Restaurant, and as I took a seat at the bar a group of businessmen began chatting with me. The group was comprised of mostly paunchy, balding older men and one young guy. They ended up buying me dinner and it turned out to be a pretty fun evening. The younger guy who wasn't drinking drove me home. He was a perfect gentleman. He walked me to my door and without any physical overtures he invited me out to dinner the next day. He was polite and respectful... or so I thought. As we began dating it turned out that he was a liar. He somehow neglected to inform me that he was married. He was in his late teens early twenties at best, a "devout" Pentecostal. Marrying young was just part of the territory. These were the kind of Pentecostals who were also known as "holy rollers." They would take to the aisles of the church and "roll" down them, overtaken by the Holy Spirit.

After a few dates Holy Roller Boy and I became intimate. It.... he was awful. I mean schoolboy, jack hammer, painful, awful. On his way out the door after our one and only encounter, he silently placed a one hundred dollar bill on my dresser. I in turn lost my mind! Apparently one of the guys he was with the night we met decided I was a prostitute. He had given Holly Roller boy the money to buy me. I shredded the bill and told him where to go. I needed that hundred dollars. I was only making minimum wage, but I was not for sale. My Promise remained intact with the shredding of that bill.

A couple of days later Holly Roller Boy's wife showed up at my door. This is how I found out he was married. This beautiful, young (almost my age) girl attired in a Holly-Hobby-like dress to the ankles was in my doorway, standing with tears in her eyes begging me to speak with her. As I let her in I remember admiring her beautiful silky brown hair that hung past her derriere. Clearly it had never been cut. I had no idea what to expect, I let her in because she wasn't in any way aggressive. She was soft spoken. She was gentle and humble. I on the other hand was mortified and angry. Angry that I didn't know he was married. I wanted to kill him, and not just for lying about his marital status. I wanted to throttle him for what he had done to this beautiful, gentle girl. She tearfully explained to me that they were both virgins when they married and that they had never so much as kissed anyone else. She told me how she hated his touch and asked if I felt the same. She thought there was something wrong with her. She asked me if I had had many lovers. She hoped I could tell her the secret to being a good lover. Here I was fifteen brushing sixteen and she maybe sixteen or seventeen, and I was to become her teacher?? How odd life can be.

I told her the truth. I told her he was a horrible lover and that love making should be gentle and kind. I told her passion should not be rough and painful AND that he was an awful kisser. I could see the relief in her eyes. She told me they already had one child and another on the way. Pentecostal girl also told me that she hated his touch but loved him. I told her that she needed to be honest with him and find a way to connect through that honesty; like I was a relationship guru. Just call me "Dear Abby." Again, life is odd.

31 THE OLD CRONY

I stayed away from the Black Angus after that and found a bar that was not too far from my apartment. This place was not as nice as the Black Angus but it beat sitting in my dark, depressing, wood-paneled studio alone. My new hang-out was a dance club featuring a nightly wet t-shirt contest (I know, classy). It was the first time I had seen one and the bouncers were trying to get me to participate, telling me I was a shoe-in for the cash prize. I refused. Not my thing, but I stayed for the dancing and fun. After my B52 night alcohol was much less attractive to me. I enjoyed just being out and in control. There was an old guy who kept trying to buy me drinks, but all I would order was a coke. He could tell I was young and broke. It wasn't really rocket science. He invited me to dinner, and well, for a free meal I was in. What's the worst that could happen? One would think that I would have learned my lesson. I think I felt safe because the bouncers at the club knew him.

He was a giant of a man that drove a big Cadillac and he was "that guy," the one going through a mid-life crisis, only he was well past middle age. He wore a ton of gold chains on his hairy chest that were displayed within his mostly unbuttoned shirt. As if that was not enough, his outfit was finished off with a huge, gaudy pinky ring. I don't remember his name, but I do remember that he was trying to "refine" me with old scotch. I took a sip and was anything but impressed; I hated it. The food, however, was great, and I wolfed it down like it was my last supper. As I was earning very little money at the arcade, food was not always, or ever in abundance. All in all dinner was fine, he spoke and I ate. He didn't seem to notice that I wasn't contributing to the conversation. He went on and on about his travels and bragging about all of the property he owned. Yawn.

On the way back to my place he abruptly pulled the car over; "get in the back" was all he said. It was an order, not a request. I was startled and immediately began to plan my exit. As I looked around I realized that we were in the middle of nowhere, there were no cars passing by, nothing. I refused to move from my seat, telling him I was tired and just wanted to go home. I thought he might try to convince me to change my mind and ultimately drive me home. Instead, he got out of the car, walked over to the passenger side and opened my door. My mind was racing. I felt sick to my stomach. Maybe he was going to leave me here, alone on a dark road. I had no idea where I was, I wished I had paid attention. "Please just take me home, I don't want to get in the back. Please can you just take me home?" As the words were falling from my lips he dragged me out of the front and placed me across the back seat like I was a rag-doll. I lay pinned under his heavy body; his breath reeked of scotch. He was sweating profusely, his beads of sweat falling on my face. I was frozen; I didn't fight him at all. I just laid there, my tears mixing with his sweat as he penetrated me. When it was over he instructed me to return to the passenger seat. I stared numbly out the window as he drove me back to my studio apartment. I never went back to that bar again. I sat for days in the dark in my quiet studio apartment, embracing the safety. I lost my job and didn't care. I just sat. A week later the cable guy showed up.

32 THE CABLE GUY

His name was Glenn. He was 6'2 with blond hair, blue eyes and a Travolta dimple in his chin. He hooked up the cable, and after a bit of small talk he asked me to dinner. We went to a restaurant that was a notch above Denny's. Over dinner I learned he was 26, played in a band, and was a roadie on the side. He lived in Baton Rouge and Lake Charles was part of his regular territory. The night was young and we decided to take a bottle of vino to the beach. We sat on a blanket under the stars, drinking the cheap wine, kissing and talking until dawn. My favourite part of the evening was that he never tried to cross the line. He was respectful, considerate and best of all he made me laugh. I felt safe and valued. I felt that he liked me and wanted to know me. I could not tell you what we talked about only that we never ran out of conversation. After our date Glenn ended up taking more work in Lake Charles and we began dating with regularity. We took the time to get to know one another and it was beautiful. We fell in love slowly, without a care in the world. As we fell deeper into one another we began to hate being so far apart. We decided that we would move in together. I happily packed my bags and settled into Glen's house in Baton Rouge.

Glen had a cute little two bedroom house that he rented with a guy named Mike. As I settled in Glenn found a better job working nine-to-five for an electrical company. My job was to keep house. Life was really good. We got along really well, and more importantly, we had great fun. We went to Crawfish boils, concerts, football games, movies, or nowhere at all. We didn't have a lot, but we were in love, well, as in love as I could be. In my heart I was completely in, but it would be many years before I would truly understand what real romantic love felt like. It would be many years before I could obliterate the numb to be able to give and receive love fully.

Nonetheless, I loved this life. I loved being "little Suzy homemaker" aka playing house. I was happy except for the part where I felt like a liar. I hated keeping my secrets. I hated hiding my true identity. I didn't want to continue lying about my age, my name and my past; but lie I did. Glenn knew something was off and he would question things, Me. The stories of my past I would tell were a combination of mine and Lawrie's past. It was my way of carrying her with me. I imagine there were inconsistencies even though I shared as little as possible. I only shared "my past" when asked. I stuck to the only child story, my parents were dead and I had no surviving family for the most part. I remember one time when he found a compact of mine that had the initials M.F. on the lid; he asked me who that stood for. Were those my "real" initials? What was my real name? He was really digging his heels into me. I stood in my usual silence. Eyes to the floor, but without tears or fear. I stood trying to figure out how to respond until it dawned on me that the initials were Max Factor! What a relief to have dodged that bullet, phew. It makes me laugh now to think of that moment. Here he was, he was right and could have broken me in that moment. I wanted to break. Living the life of a made-up person was lonely. Not being able to share a real past, a real life was lonely; even if it was a past best forgotten.

I have a feeling that if I had told him the truth he would have tried to make contact with my "family." Not to throw me under a bus, but to try to make things right with them. People have difficulty understanding that not all families are meant to have relationships. Some things simply cannot be fixed. Glenn would find out my true identity down the road... but we're not there yet.

Things began to change when Mike, Glenn's roommate moved out. Mike was a horse's arse but he did pay half of the bills. He was arrogant and thought he was g-d's gift to women. I disliked him, but always played nice in the sandbox. He spent a lot of his time at his ginger haired girlfriend's house. She was tall and thin with big boobs, kind of a trophy for him I think. I liked her, but she was uber jealous of everyone. Turns out she had every right to be, he was an absolute snake. One day while Glenn was at work, he tried to give me a tonsillectomy with his tongue. I managed to escape him and in a pre-emptive strike he told Glenn that I came on to him. I told Glenn what had occurred, but I could feel the mistrust. As a child I was raised to believe that everything bad that occurred was my fault. I always felt guilty about everything. There was no logic to this feeling. Even though I knew I did nothing to bring on Mike's advances, I questioned whether I did or not. At any rate, Mike moved in with his girlfriend leaving us with double the expenses. Time for Valentine to get a job.

I found a job at a nearby clothing store. It was a small family owned department store that carried low-end apparel for the entire family. Think Big Lots meets camouflage hunting garb. My boss was nothing to write home about. He was as low-end as the store, skinny with dark hair and a straggly beard. Appearance not withstanding he was easy to work for. Very low-key. He would even drive me home on his motorcycle on a regular basis. As a thank you for saving me from public transportation I would invite him in for a beer. I thought nothing of it. My heart was Glenn's and he knew I had a boyfriend. One day Glenn came home from work to find us sitting on the sofa. Glenn had to explain to me why it was inappropriate for me to have a man over when he wasn't home. That was the last time I took a ride from my boss, but apparently the neighbors told Glenn he had been over several times, which was true. What was not true were the assumptions made. With the stress that this was causing I quit my job to keep my boyfriend; we agreed he would take overtime for us to be able to make ends meet.

33 CHILD WITH CHILD

I was excited to be sharing our first Christmas together and decked the house out with lights and a tree. As a Jewish girl I was always envious of people that celebrated Christmas. I loved the pretty lights and never understood why we didn't decorate for Hanukah. My second favourite thing to the decor was the baking. I loved to bake and decorate cakes and cookies. My "Suzy homemaker" life was carefree and I was very content. I could have stayed there forever.

Christmas and New Years came and went, filled with get-togethers and cheap champagne toasts. It was now less than a month after my seventeenth birthday and things took an unexpected turn. I began to notice some changes in my body. My breasts were tender and I swear I felt little butterflies in my belly. Glenn commented that I was gaining weight in a "watch that" sort of way. I was shocked at the way he spoke to me; he never critiqued me... not like that anyway. I was pretty tiny and any weight gain would have been very apparent. It took missing a couple of periods before it dawned on me that I was pregnant. I had no clue as to whether Glenn would be happy or angry. I also didn't know how I felt. As the realization hit, I made a better than usual dinner and prepared to tell him. I was hoping for a magical movie moment, reasoning that we were in love and a child is a gift. I also knew there was a possibility he would not be happy given our financial situation.

We were lying in bed watching television in our sweats. My head on his chest, my mind spinning as I tried to work up the courage to tell him. I thought about why we had never talked about birth control. I don't know if he assumed I was on the pill or simply didn't care. Before I could open my mouth a commercial came on advertising diapers, the perfect seg-way... or so I thought. The next thing I knew Glenn was saying "I think babies are useless and never want to have any." Those words are seared in my brain. I laid there stunned, fighting back tears trying to make sense of what he had just said. I felt like I had been sucker punched in the stomach. I was immediately nauseous and it had nothing to do with my pregnancy. I asked him why he felt that way, what he meant. The conversation went nowhere. The only thing I was left with was that he never wanted to be a father, period.

34 KNOW WHEN TO FOLD 'EM

In the week that followed I had to tell him. It's not like I could keep it under wraps for long. The first words that fell out of Glenn's mouth, word rather, was "abortion." And then, ok......WE will get an abortion. WE. Like it was his body that would be lying on a table feeling a life being sucked out of it. Anger overtook my hurt. I told him under no uncertain terms that I didn't want an abortion and that I likewise wanted nothing from him. I planned to move to Columbus and have my baby there. Why Columbus? Do you remember hippie girl, whom I met in the student housing area when I was selling "Amazing 901?" You know, the one that told me I could come back and crash anytime? Never mind that I didn't know her last name or have her phone number. I was certain I could find her house and just show up. Glenn reluctantly drove me to the bus station, all the while asking me not to leave. He kept telling me he that loved me and we can just have an abortion. I just kept thinking, repeating in my mind "we" could have an abortion. "We." As if he was carrying our baby. I think I stopped loving him in that very moment. I know I stopped respecting him. I no longer felt safe or protected by him. Getting on the bus was easy. As he was holding me and telling me I didn't have to go, all I wanted was for him to stop touching me. I started to hate him, I wanted him to stop talking. In that moment I felt that I never wanted to hear his voice ever again. I boarded the bus and didn't even bother to look back at him. I stared straight ahead, I could see Glenn looking at me from the corner of my eye. I sat stoic, with angry tears burning in my eyes. I would not let them drop. He was no longer worth one of my tears. Numb.

My decision not to abort my baby had nothing to do with my beliefs. My decision had everything to do with the fact that I could feel this being fluttering inside of me; for the first time in my life I felt like I wasn't alone. Sad that I didn't want my baby for the right reasons at the time. My baby was going to fill me, love me, need me, and ensure I would never be alone again. It was all about me and my needs in those early moments. I didn't know it at the time, but my baby was going to save my life. Not because she was going to love me, but because of the way that I would fall in love with her. She would force me to love myself, to take care of myself, so that I could take care of her.

35 A TASTE OF MOTHERHOOD

I arrived at a bus station in Columbus, Ohio on a very cold winter night. I didn't consider the temperature change and only had a light jacket. Let's face it, planning and preparation were not my strong suits. I had to layer the few shirts I had under the jacket to keep from freezing. It did not take long for me to figure out that I had no idea where I was and nowhere to go. I didn't have an address or a concept of how far away the Ohio State University student houses were. I also did not have very much money with me. Glenn paid for my bus ticket and gave me what he could spare. I was seventeen, approximately three months pregnant, exhausted, cold, and alone. I sat on a bench in the bus depot trying to figure out my next move. A kid, a boy around my age, started talking to me, and it wasn't long before we came to the conclusion we were in the same boat. We split a taxi and found a motel room in the kind of hood where drug deals were taking place on street corners in plain sight. The next day my new friend tried to help me find hippie girl's house, to no avail. We walked up and down the streets around the university for hours. I finally had to acknowledge that all of the houses looked the same.

Fearing homelessness and knowing that abandoned buildings in the winter were not going to be an option, I needed to find a job, fast! I perused the want ads and quickly landed a live-in nanny job in an area that was filled with welfare families and subsidized housing. I was hired by a little boy's grandmother who as it turned out was the boy's legal guardian. Both her son and grandson lived there with her. The little boy's name was Robert and he was dealt a tough hand very early on. His mother was a drug addict who had left shortly after his birth. His father floated in and out of his life without much interest in the little guy. Robert was around 5 years old and had seen many nannies come and go by the time I arrived on the scene. His skin was as pale as a Dresden doll; the contrast made his brown eyes almost seem black. He had thick, wavy dark hair and was a slight little thing. He didn't eat well and he was a painfully quiet little soul. I loved him immediately, I was him. I was paid twenty five dollars in cash per week plus room and board. I wasn't showing yet and didn't tell them I was pregnant out of fear of not being hired. I figured I would just cross that bridge when I had to, having a warm bed and food was my only real focus at this point.

As I settled in I wrote Glenn a letter to let him know that I was ok. While I no longer wanted to be with him, I did want my baby to have a father. I told him, begged him to be a father to our baby. I told him that I didn't want any money. I just wanted our baby to know him. In the letter I gave him the phone number where I was living and told him if he wanted to be a father to call me. A couple of weeks later Glenn called. When I heard his voice I felt hopeful. I thought that his call meant he was going to step up for our baby. Glenn told me that he wanted me to come back. He told me that he loved and missed me. He wanted us to be together, I just had to do one thing. Have an abortion. Click, I hung up.

36 THE NANNY

My job description included taking Robert to and from school, helping with homework, doing laundry and preparing meals. The first few weeks I was there Robert's father was away. His grandmother worked and kept the roof over our heads. One day as Robert and I were sitting at the kitchen table working on a school project his father walked in. I was startled at the site of this tall, fat, redneck of a man. It took me a moment to figure out who he was based on photographs I had seen on the mantel. He had been gone for weeks, and Robert barely looked up to acknowledge his dad. His father also barely acknowledged Robert, no smile, no affection... nothing. After his return home Robert's father spent his days working on his motorcycles, contributing little to the house or to Robert for that matter. I felt so sad for Robert. He was such an affectionate, beautiful little boy. I did my best to be his mommy. I read to him, I watched over him during school recess, took him to the park and baked him his favorite chocolate chip cookies. I would do anything to keep him happy, to see him smile.

Upon Robert's fathers return I quickly understood why there was a revolving door on the nannies. Robert's grandmother was hiring us to be his father's girlfriend. After a few days of being home he began to impose himself on me. Coming into my room in the middle of the night to "cuddle". I kept him at bay for as long as I could, but he knew he had me in a corner. As my pregnancy began to show he capitalized on my vulnerability and raped me. I wanted so badly to leave, but Robert would get teary eyed when I would drop him off at school. He began asking me if I would be picking him up. He would also ask me if I was going to leave like the other nannies. This little 5 year old knew the score. I promised him I would stay. Trapped. I was trapped by my heart and my pregnancy. Who was going to hire a very apparent pregnant girl?

Months passed and I was around 7 months pregnant without benefit of pre-natal care; I was desperately trying to hold-on for myself and Robert. While I was showing I had not gained nearly enough weight. I looked to be five months along and was wearing size seven jeans comfortably. A mother of one of Robert's classmates asked me how far along I was and was shocked at my response. She told me I needed to see a doctor and take better care of myself. She told me stories about the other girls who had worked for Robert's grandmother. Apparently they wouldn't just leave. Robert's father would get bored of them and kick them out with no concern of where they landed. She told me that eventually they would stop paying me. I told her that I had not been paid in over a month. When I asked about my pay Robert's grandmother said I should just be grateful that

I had a roof over my head, adding that had she known she would have never hired a pregnant girl.

I don't remember the name of the mom from Robert's class. I do remember she was young and had at least 5 children ranging from baby to 17.

Her house was always clean, her children were well cared for and she accepted, she knew, that this was her destiny; living in low rent housing and having babies. I can remember her eldest boy vividly. He took on the role of daddy in the house. He knew he was a role model for his younger siblings. He was a boy with a bright future in spite of living in a welfare home. He worked two jobs, earned straight A's and had a plan to get himself and his family out of the hood. I hope he did. I have faith that he did.

37 A BROKEN PROMISE

As much as I didn't want to leave Robert I knew I could not have my baby in that house. I could not allow Robert's father to continue abusing me. I had to put my baby first. Telling Robert I had to break my promise was one of the hardest things I have ever had to do. I held onto him as we cried. I promised to visit him at school during recess. I kept that promise until he had a new nanny, until I felt he didn't need me anymore.

I moved onto Welfare Mom's couch as a temporary fix. I was only there about a week when her boyfriend came over to offer up his place. He was about to go to jail on a drug charge and had been given time to settle his affairs before serving his sentence. He told us that he had paid the rent on his studio apartment; it would be empty for the remainder of the month and I was welcome to it. I moved in with nothing more than a small suitcase filled with clothing that thanks to Welfare Mom were beginning not to fit my now rapidly growing belly. We went down to the local food pantry and they gave us each a bag filled with food. I can remember there was mostly pasta and canned vegetables in it; less than adequate nutrition for a pregnant girl who wasn't taking prenatal vitamins. As luck would not have it, a few days into my stay the electricity was turned off. It's kind of difficult to cook pasta if you can't boil the water. Speaking of water... there was no longer any hot water. No electricity equals no hot water heater. Had I not been pregnant this would not have been so bad. Think about it. In comparison to abandoned buildings, this would have been a breeze.

Fortunately for me Welfare Mom knew the public assistance ropes. She was born into the system. She took me to Planned Parenthood and they hooked me up with pre-natal care, WIC (a program to provide nutrition for women and children) and a better food bank. Planned Parenthood sent me, the little Jewish girl, to a Christian based unwed mothers-to-be foundation. The foundation placed pregnant teenage girls in homes while they figured out whether to keep their babies or adopt them out, encouraging the latter.

38 ENDLESS LOVE

I landed in the home of Larry and Diane, a couple in their late thirties/ early forties. They had a sweet eleven year old daughter who became like a little sister to me. Diane was a nursing student who in addition to school was also holding down a full-time job. Larry was working full time and their daughter would often come home to an empty house. They needed someone to be around and wanted to help a girl like me. It was an ideal set up for all.

Diane was gone most of the time and Larry told me they lived together out of convenience. He said they were more like good friends and that their arrangement was good for their daughter and their finances. Friends or not, he and Diane had sex every Thursday night like clockwork. Other than the Thursday night sex thing they always slept in their own bedrooms. It was all very confusing for me. Keep in mind this was over thirty years ago, friends or exes with benefits were not a thing. Larry also told me that he loved pregnant women. He told me I was beautiful. I liked his attention. I liked him. I loved their daughter and I didn't want to leave. I also had nowhere to go. All of that said, Larry never made me feel uncomfortable. He was nothing like Robert's father.

As Diane was gone most of the time, Larry and I were alone night after night. He was always doing sweet things for me. Bringing me flowers or ice cream. Taking me to the movies... to dinner. Like we were a couple... like I was carrying his baby, a baby he wanted. Eventually something developed and we weren't hiding it. He still had sex with Diane on Thursdays, which drove me crazy... and kept me confused. We were out in the open. Why would she still want sex with him? Why was he still having sex with her? It didn't add up. And well...We... I thought she knew about us. We were in no way hiding our relationship. Larry and I would sit on the couch as close as a couple would and she didn't bat an eye for the longest time; then one evening, out of the blue she commented to him about our affection. She told him she didn't like it. As a result we quickly altered our behaviour. Larry said it was just to not hurt her feelings. Here I was 17, involved with a forty year old married-ish man and about to give birth any day. Larry was attending Lamaze classes (which Diane encouraged) with me, he would kiss my belly and speak to my baby. It was as if I was carrying his baby and he was more than happy to take on the role of daddy. He was excited for the birth. We shopped for my unborn baby together. He bought the basinet and the stroller... diapers... onesies.

I am trying to get in touch with what was going through my head during this period and I cannot connect, I've got nothing. It was just an odd arrangement with an even odder romantic relationship.

It was brutally hot as August set in. In fact that summer had broken all of the heat records with temperatures running between 95 and 100 degrees Fahrenheit. I had gone from a size seven jeans to huge. My body was still thin but my belly was ginormous. You could not tell I was pregnant unless you caught a side view or front view of me.

It was August 19th, 1983 and I had just gone to bed. Between the heat outside and the life-size heater inside of me, the fan in my room was not helping to cool any part of me down. I was tossing and turning trying desperately to sleep; and then it happened... just prior to midnight my water broke.

I came out of the bedroom, dripping and a little confused, Diane and Larry were sitting on the couch watching a movie. Diane took one look at me and ran to grab a bunch of towels. We walked out to the car together and Diane laid towels on the seat as Larry started to the car. She helped settle me into the passenger seat and told me she couldn't wait to meet my baby. Off we went as I sat in a state of numb and shock. I knew I was going to have a baby, but in spite of the Lamaze classes I was in a kind of "what is happening?" fog. We arrived at the hospital and waited for the contractions to begin. The nurses had me walk in an effort to avoid inducing labor. I walked for a couple hours on and off until the first pain took hold. It would be twelve hours of hard labor with little relief between contractions. I wanted to have a natural birth, but I was exhausted and could no longer handle the pain. I was given something that allowed me to doze for the sixty or so seconds in between the feeling of my insides being ripped apart.

As they wheeled me from the labor room to the delivery room my baby's head began to come out, she was born on the way to the delivery room. She was a blue-grey colour and it seemed forever before she cried. I watched as they took her over to the bassinet, I remember thinking it's a baby, a real baby. It was absolutely surreal. I had a baby. My daughter was born on August 20th at 12:22 pm weighing a beautifully normal seven pounds, eight ounces. A baby girl that I would name Jade after the movie "Endless Love." I loved Brooke Shields, the name and the movie. It's ironic that I would name my little daughter after a movie. My mother named me after the Alfred Hitchcock movie entitled "Marnie." Irrefutable evidence that some history repeats.

In 1983 hospitals kept mother and baby for three days. If you were indigent, on welfare or a minor, social services would visit and assess what services were needed. As my social worker came in, so did the questions. My case worker advised me about the law. *A law that I was not going to like.* When I registered with the Christian pregnant teens foundation that placed me I had to give them my real age to receive their help. That's how social services knew I wasn't eighteen. When a minor gives birth in the state of Ohio, social services was required to report the birth to the minor's parents. While social services and the Christian foundation had my real age they did not have my real name. As I began to come to grips with the fact that my daughter's birth certificate would have my alias I knew I had to come clean. For her and I to receive the benefits I had to come clean. I would need to support my little baby girl. This also meant having to tell Larry and Diane that I had been lying to them. These people were nothing but kind to me and took me in during my darkest hour; in return I had repaid them by lying. I cannot describe the fear and guilt that was taking hold. I would have run if it had only been me, but I was trapped.

39 MY NAME IS MARNIE…
PLEASE DON'T BE ANGRY

I gave my case worker my real name and told her where I was from. I also told her that I was a runaway and begged her not to tell my mother where I was. She took the information and told me she would be in touch without addressing my request.

Larry excitedly picked me up from the hospital oohing and awing over Jade. On the ride home I was a mix of exhaustion, numb and anxiety… dread. My mind was spinning. How was I going to come clean? Diane greeted us at the door, giving me a big hug. She had the bassinet all ready for Jade and was beyond excited to cuddle her. Diane told me if I was too tired she would be happy to get up in the middle of the night for Jade's feedings. I was exhausted and wished that were an option but I was breastfeeding. I wanted to be as close to my baby as I could. I wanted, *needed*, to give her the love and nurturing I had never received from my own mother.

We ate dinner as Jade slept in the bassinet next to the table. I had no appetite, the food tasted like cardboard to me. All I wanted to do was run. I wanted to take my baby and disappear. I was terrified of what was going to happen with my mother. I was afraid I was going to be kicked out for all of the lies I had told them. After dinner we went and sat on the couch. I can picture the scene like a slow-motion movie.

Larry told me he knew about my real name, the social worked had told him when he picked me up. I reluctantly, fearfully began to tell them my story. I expected Diane and Larry to be angry and disappointed, I thought they would hate me. I braced myself for the very worst. As I told my story they both had tears in their eyes, Diane came over and embraced me. Funny, she was crying and I never shed a tear. I was lost in numb, and I felt no sorrow for myself. It would be a great many years until I would actually cry for myself, that little girl and the youth that had been stolen from her. For the life of me I couldn't figure out why Diane was crying. I was bad, I was a liar. I remember thinking, "Why are you being kind and loving?" It never dawned on me that anyone would feel bad for me or believe me to be anything but bad. I was unfamiliar with compassion. It was a relief, but it was also very, very uncomfortable. My mother had me convinced that I was bad, that I was worthless and undeserving of compassion let alone love.

Diane and Larry both responded by saying things like "We are so sorry for all that you have been through. It's a miracle that you have survived and turned out so well." I was very, very confused; I was also very, very relieved. They weren't going to kick me out. My baby and I were going to be okay.

40 FORCIBLY FOUND

As social services began the process of informing Evil One about my baby they could not find a missing child report anywhere within the Miami Police Department. The social worker was surprised, and I could tell that she felt bad for me. I had told her nobody would care that I was gone; now I had proof. I told her there was no reason for the notification. I was hoping she would let it go, but she had to obey the law. I had no choice. To receive benefits I had to give her my mother's name and phone number.

As it turns out a report was filed by my mother, but because she was not following-up with the police it fell behind the reports of children whose parents were actively looking. The whole time that I lived in North Miami and South Beach I was within fifteen miles of my house. In the early months I was within five miles. Knowing how close I was during that period and not being found supported my feeling that nobody cared. I did not want to be found, but at the same time how could they not find me if they were really looking? The 7 Eleven was only a few blocks from one of Pop's drug stores. The Seville was three miles from another of his pharmacies, and only six miles from their house.

My caseworker spoke with Evil One and called me to ask me to phone her. She told me that my mother wanted me home, that she loved me. She loved me? Words she rarely spoke to me. When she did speak those words she was high, drunk or both. Larry and Diane said that they would sit with me while I called. They assured me that I was safe and encouraged me to at least have a conversation with her. I didn't want to, but I felt cornered and powerless to refuse. Truth be told they could have asked me to jump off of a bridge, "no" was not in my vocabulary. Serving my needs was not a skill I had developed, that's why I always ran. That is how I said "no."

Jade was seven days old when I found myself in a three-way phone conversation with Pop and my mother. They were elated to hear my voice. This would be the first time I would hear my mother say she loves me without being under the influence. I believed her, I needed to believe her. She wanted me to come home. She asked tons of questions about Jade and told me she would take care of us. Everything I always wanted, needed to hear from her. I felt like I was dreaming. Even with all I knew about her and had experienced by her hand, I didn't have a moment of doubt. I bought into her... hook, line and sinker. I bought into her like I was a potential beau she was luring in.

41 HOMECOMING...SORT OF

My mother was leaving for Montreal the next day for my brother's engagement party. Pop handled all of the arrangements and flew my ten day old baby and I to Miami where I would meet him and my grandparents in the airport. It was all very surreal. They threw their arms around me and I was like a statue. I think I was in shock. In ten days time I had given birth to a new baby, became Marnie again, and was now reuniting with the very people that I had run from. There was no time to process. Numb.

Pop and I flew to Montreal alone. My grandparents would be flying the next day. He spent the three hour flight updating me on what I had missed in the three plus years I had been gone. The only topic he avoided was Ernesto. Ernesto was the only topic I had any real interest in. He was the only one who I had not run from, and given the opportunity I would have run to. When I asked where Ernesto was and if he knew I was back, Pop changed the subject. After all of the updates Pop chose to share he also told me that I picked a good time to run away. He said they were running low on money and weren't sure how they were going to send me back to boarding school. I picked a good time to run away?! Did I also pick a good time to be raped?! To starve for days?! To be homeless and hopeless?! I will never forget his words and the matter of fact way in which he spoke them. I sat holding my baby girl... letting her comfort me, rocking us both. Numb, but for her warmth.

Pop's declaration along with my mother's actions on the day that I ran were spinning in my psyche. The truth behind my mother's decision regarding boarding school was out in the open. Her making me return "home" is what set the three year run in motion, forever stealing what was left of my youth... and my innocence. More likely than not it could have all been prevented with the truth. The truth could have allowed Ernesto's family to help, and they would have. Money was no object to them. This was a family that flew from Caracas to New York just to meet me. We all stayed at the Plaza together and ate with Venezuelan ambassadors at the 21 club. They took me shopping at Tiffany's and had Ernesto pick out a beautiful necklace for me. They absolutely would have stepped in. All that mattered was their son's happiness. I sat there, deflated by his words. "I picked a good time to run."

42 THE MORE THINGS CHANGE....

It was all very surreal. Everyone welcomed me back, hugging and kissing me, the statue. The only time I softened was in my mother's embrace. So unfamiliar and everything I had longed for. We even exchanged "I love you" words several times within the embrace. I was putty in her arms.

Everyone was of course ooohing and awing over Jade. They asked minimal questions for the most part. The reception from some of my cousins, who were close to my age, was not quite as warm and fuzzy. One in particular was very angry with me and gave me the cold shoulder. I had never fought with her in my life. Renee was my little cousin, I adored her when we were kids. Hell, we were both still kids. She was around thirteen and I was seventeen. I find it ironic that when I returned "home" she would be the same age that I was when I ran. I could not understand why she was angry with me anymore than she would ever understand why I ran. To her my mother was fun and great to be around. An easy opinion to have when you see her fourteen days a year, a few days at a time. As I settled into my Aunt's house I went into Renee's room, immediately noticing a couple of sculptures on a shelf in her bookcase. My late father had given them to me a few months before he passed away. There were very few things I had left from him. I loved those sculptures; they were happy and simple, smiling little children on swing sets cast in bronze.

I asked her if I could have them back and she refused. This girl who lived a two million dollar home and had every material item you could imagine. She did not need or want for anything. Her mom was loving, her dad a very active participant in her life. She had everything, and she could not give me back what was mine even after I explained why I wanted them. I pleaded with her, I tearfully begged her to return the sculptures. She refused and no one intervened. As far as I know she still has them.

It took a little over a week for my mother to morph into her old self, into Evil One. We had my brother's engagement party to go to and she took me to the hairdresser. I was so excited to go until almost all of my hair was cut off. She gave the directive and I complied. I was outfitted according to her standards and my silence set-in as per usual. It was if no time had passed, I had never been missing. We picked up our "relationship" right where we left off.

Witnessing what was happening, my aunt invited to me to live at her house with Jade. The only condition was that I would have to attend counselling. I desperately wanted to stay on, but Evil One said no. She knew that therapy would enable me to "out" her and she needed to find a way to silence me... quickly. She informed my aunt that I would be returning to Miami. That was that. As if I had never been on my own, the ever silent "good little girl" went back to Miami. As we pulled up to the house my mother informed me that my room had been made into a guest room. I learned from Pop that it was converted less than a year after I left.

The only evidence that I had ever lived in the house at all was in a suitcase tucked away in the garage. The suitcase contained random items like sheet music, a couple of outfits and a sculpture that I had created out of soap stone while I was in summer camp. The rest of my belongings had been given to my cousins, sold or donated to goodwill.

I lived in Evil One's house for exactly one week before Pop came to me to suggest other accommodations. There had been no conflict. There had also been little interaction. Evil One was either holed up in her bedroom or out. The only interest she had was in my baby. She showered Jade with affection. It was such a foreign thing to witness. She was actually soft with her. I had never seen or experienced that side of her. Nonetheless, Evil One was having a hard time with me being under the same roof.

I went to live in a villa on the grounds of one of the hotel properties that my grandfather was a part owner of in Miami Beach. Pop gave me a part-time job at one of his drug stores and I would bring Jade to work with me. I loved living on the ocean and would often begin my day taking in the sunrise while sitting on the sand with Jade in my arms. I was settling into my new apartment, but life was anything but good. I was struggling. I knew that my relationship with Evil One was not going to get better. She didn't want the responsibility for me the first time around, let alone now. She was relieved by my departure and revelled in the attention given to her as the poor mother of a child who had disappeared. My presence was threatening her perfect appearance.

Not only had I run, I had returned as a teenage mother. According to her standards (and everyone else's in 1983) that was the sort of thing that only happens in trailer parks, not in Jewish, upper middle-class homes.

Somehow this silent girl worked up the nerve to ask my mother about Ernesto. I had already asked my grandparents and brother and no one would give me a straight answer. Evil <ne told me that he had moved on shortly after I ran away. She said he would not care that I was found. She confirmed that she had his contact information and refused to give it to me. As it was 1983 there was no Facebook, in fact there was also no internet. I had no way to find him. She further told me he would not want me. She

told me I was damaged goods (which I already knew). Who would want a seventeen year old with a baby?

My Aunt continually badgered Evil One and insisted she take me to counselling. She caved under the pressure and finally took me, twice. Evil One sat in on my first session, explaining to the therapist that I was an unmanageable child and had run away constantly before finally staying away for three years. She went on and on about all that I had put her through. I sat there, eyes to the floor... by now you know the theme. The counsellor began to ask me questions and because of my silence she asked Evil One to step out. I still told her nothing. Ok, not nothing, just nothing of substance. Evil One had told me the following prior to my first session, "I'm paying the therapist, she will and does tell me everything you say." The counsellor went out of her way to tell me the opposite right in front of E.O. No matter, I was too afraid of Evil One to believe her. Evil One dropped me off at one more session after that. I don't remember what I talked about, but I do remember that I said nothing about Evil One. I would not dare to discuss her. When she picked me up she told me that the therapist told her I was trashing her and that I needed to take responsibility for my actions. I never went back. Evil One had won again. After that she told my aunt I didn't want to go and that was the end of therapy.

It would be six years after my return "home" until I would finally walk, not run away from my mother. With the love and support of my ex-husband I found my voice and cut all ties. By this point Jade was around six; I had been married to an extremely violent man whom I divorced, but not before he gave me my beautiful son, James who was now in his two's. It would be the birth of my youngest daughter, Daniella that would be the catalyst for my finally committing to therapy to move through and past the trauma of my childhood. It would be over twenty years until I would finally face the demons of the memories of my life on the streets: That is what writing this book has made me do.

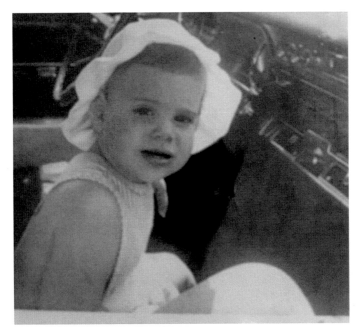

Marnie, age unknown

Marnie and her half-brother Steven

Marnie's school photo from Roslyn Elementary in Westmount, Montreal Approximateley 6 years old (already a runner)

Marnie's 6th birthday the summer before the big bus run

Marnie, 8 & 1/2 years old, along with Daddy (Lenny)
and Evil One

Marnie, Age 10
school photo from
William Jennings Bryan
Elementary School
in North Miami, Florida

Marnie and Gucci,
(A few months before she was given away)

**Cheshire Academy yearbook photo a few months before the
"final run"**

17 year old Marnie with her Daughter Jade,
age twelve days first visit with the maternal family since Marnie
went MISSING over 3 years earlier

Mother's Day 2000
Top to bottom
Jade, age 16
James, Age 13
Marnie, Age 34
Daniella, Age 8

PART II

The truth always comes out. After my return home I was told how bad I was, how angry everyone was with me. How people had written me off. What I put everyone through. My mother led me to believe that everyone hated me and was angry with me. I believed everyone knew I was bad. It would be a very long time before I would realize the truth, even longer before I would receive proof of the truth. My first realization came from my ex-husband. When he found out I had run away from home at thirteen his words to me were "no child runs away from a good home, no child runs away without good reason." He was the first person in my life to validate me. He was also the first person who ever asked me if I was okay. I was around twenty two when we met and he was the first person to validate me. He was the man that I would end up growing up with for the next thirteen years. He released me from the thought that I was damaged goods. He was the first person in my life to give me a sense of self, a sense of myself. The beginning of my becoming a confident woman is a direct result of the years I shared with him.

ERNESTO

Thirty years after my return I briefly re-united with Ernesto. His sister found me on Classmates.com. He and I are friends to this day. Sadly when we re-united we quickly realized that we were no longer those sweet little innocent children. It breaks my heart to know the way I broke his. It breaks my heart to know the way that I changed the course of his life. He was never angry with me, not even when I ran. I all but ruined his life and he still holds absolute love for me. He filled in many blanks for me and shed light on Evil One's lies. I learned that he and his family had NEVER stopped looking for me. In fact, his parents worked with Interpol and hired two full-time private detectives to look for me. They kept them on my case for over two years.

Ernesto was not informed of my return and if he had been he would have moved heaven and earth for a chance to love me, to make a life with me. It was not too late when I returned home. My having a baby girl would not have changed his love for me. These are all of the words he spoke to me when we met for the first time after thirty years apart.

Almost ten years after my disappearance Ernesto married and had two children, one also named Daniella. His marriage ended in divorce and about a year after we met again he remarried. He now lives in Venezuela with his second wife and their little son.

In addition to the private detectives, he and Steven were actively looking for me together. Looking for me in the way you would expect... oh I don't know, a *mother* to look for her child. This is the part where I really do want to fry Evil One. My stomach is in knots thinking about her. I don't do numb anymore so I will have to take a moment and breathe... just breathe.

Ernesto gave up his life for almost two years (my half-brother gave up summers and holidays for one year). He did not return to boarding school. He exhaustively retraced what he thought were my steps. He ended up in brothels looking for me because someone said they thought I was being held there. Ernesto was a young man who grew up with chauffeurs and Butlers, he was grounded and extremely intelligent. He had nothing but a bright future ahead of him. Ernesto gave it all up, mimicking my life on the streets to find me. He went off the grid hoping to mirror my footsteps. He lived like a runaway in many respects. He tirelessly plastered the city with flyers. His parents gave him a year and then insisted he return to school. He tried to resume school, but left to take another year to look for me. He eventually did graduate and subsequently became a pilot.

All of that time I thought I was alone. I believed that nobody cared. I was sure that nobody would even bat an eye at my disappearance. I believed when I left I would simply be forgotten. I realize how absurd that sounds, but it is how I felt. It is what my mother drilled into me; and as you can see it is how she herself felt about me. For her I was out of sight, out of mind. I have no doubt she was happy to rid her home of my existence, and that she milked the sympathy train for as long as she could.

My classmates believed that I had been abducted and murdered. We reconnected on Facebook and these are excerpts from our actual conversations. I am not using his name, we will call him Prince, because I think he is a Prince of a guy.

Prince: "This is going to get deep, but I need some closure. Murdered... so for 30 years..Some who knew you lived with this rumor.'

"That you were killed."

Me" "Oh my gosh! Thats pretty awful. I can see how it happened. I did go missing and no one knew where I was was for 3 years."

Prince: "On march 31st this year, I was on my deathbed..and I thought of you."

"And I prayed..."

Me: "You thought of me? really?"

Prince: "And I never pray"

"Dying..."

Me: "why did you think of me? I can understand why you prayed"

Prince: "Because I knew you, and I knew what a kind person you were, and I prayed you didn't suffer, and we could talk."

"So.."

"I didn't die.."

Me: "and were talking...wowza"

"I am really touched."

"sadly I didn't really. believe anyone thought much of me back then. thank you." (Unbeknownst to Prince as I am corresponding with him I am weeping hysterically. I would fall asleep weeping from our correspondence.

Prince: "And you are alive...the 30 year rumor just has me fuckedup right now...please excuse my language."

"you my dear are a blessing"

For thirty years this Prince carried me in his heart. I can't find adequate words to express how sad and happy this made me at the same time. I wept when I thought about his pain, the pain I caused. I wept when I thought about my pain, the pain my mother caused. I wept because I was learning after all of the years that had passed, that I was important, that I was memorable.

GLENN

Glenn eventually learned the truth about my name and past. He expressed sadness for me and told me he always knew something was off. We attempted to become a family when Jade was a baby, but it didn't stick. I was too angry because I felt so abandoned by him. We no longer trusted or respected one another. We tried, but sadly it just wasn't there. He is recently divorced. He never had anymore children.

LAWRIE

I ran into Lawrie when my Jade was around a year old. Lawrie had a beautiful three year old daughter who was obviously being neglected. She had patches of hair missing from where she had been pulling it out in clumps. Lawrie was a mess, I suppose in many ways she was the same as we were when we were on the streets. She lived in an unkempt apartment and I think she was still escorting to make ends meet. She had not recovered from her time on the streets. I don't know what became of her after that, I doubt that I ever will.

MY MATERNAL FAMILY

The majority of my family was not so understanding. They were very much on the side of my mother. My cousins only knew her as the fun aunt that would land with gifts in hand and a smile on her face. They never witnessed the evil and couldn't understand why I left. I never shared any of my experiences with them. I knew I would not be believed. My brother remains disappointed and angry with me. We have no relationship. I have reached out to him, but he refuses to have anything to do with me to this day. When I broke ties with my grandparents and mother, he broke ties with me. In fact when I broke ties and confronted my mother with the past my entire family shut their doors to me. I only have a little contact with one cousin and it's superficial at best.

HOME IN THE ARMS OF MY PATERNAL FAMILY

Thanks to Facebook I connected with my younger half sister seven years ago. She opened the door to what would end up being the beginning of my relationship with my father and three other half siblings, plus aunts and cousins and a step-mother. My step-mother has become my mom, and I address her accordingly. My father filled my cup and healed most of my wounds. He validated my experiences and took ownership of his actions... or inactions. Words cannot express the respect and love I have for him. I am sure you are wondering how could I "forgive" his abandonment and worse yet the rejection of being left in his office on that day that would never be spoken of. Never; that is, until my father took ownership of me, his daughter.

He stepped up on his own and did everything in his power to make up for the lost time and experiences. My father for over three hours, without any ask on my part, took ownership of all of his past misdeeds. More importantly he did the one thing that NO ONE in my maternal family would or has ever done. He spoke the truth. Not the "truth" that would make him look good. Not the "truth" that would only "out" my mother. Just the truth, the honesty I had longed for all of my life. He stepped up and faced the music not knowing whether I would be screaming like the Sex Pistols or humming "All You Need Is Love." My father filled my cup with his love every day. The moments where he felt regret were seen in silent glances that he knew I understood and forgave. He gave me the love, family and acceptance that I had searched for my entire life. He gave me peace, and made me laugh. I am proud to call myself my father's daughter.

Sadly, tragically, he passed away three years ago. I miss him every single day. I thank the universe everyday for gifting me with his love and making me whole.

**Marnie and her father Gerry at Marnie's
1st vernisage in Old Montreal**

TIME TO STOP RUNNING

It would take me forty nine plus years and several broken relationships before I would finally realize that even when I wasn't running geographically, I was running. I run out on relationships instead of communicating my way through them. I run out on myself and I consistently create instability both emotionally and financially. Because of my life on the streets I had made it my life's work to keep myself off kilter and unhappy. I've been a transient girl committing myself to a life without solid ground.

No more. I have finally figured out that I can have a home base. I deserve a home base. Somewhere that no matter where I am or where I go I have a space that is my own to come back to. More importantly I now know that I can do that for myself. I was taught by my mother to look outside myself to have my material needs met. I was taught by her to look into myself to have my emotional needs met. I was raised to be a parasite... to have a man take care of me. I was taught that all I have to offer is the physical.

Somewhere along the way, through standing on my own two feet and through all of my broken relationships I have finally come into my own. You can NOT move forward until after you have gone backwards. To let go and move ahead you have to deal with the demons and the pain, fully; and, most importantly, head on. You have to give yourself permission to grieve, to envelop yourself in the pains of the past and bury it outside of yourself. You also have to give yourself permission not to forgive the unforgivable. Forgiveness is overrated.

It is more than okay to let yourself own un-forgiveness. The only – and I do mean only –person you have to forgive is yourself. Understand that forgiving others and letting go of anger towards them is not synonymous. You can let go of anger, and you should because the only one who cares you are angry is you. You can let go of anger and, contrary to popular belief, not forgive. My mother did horrible things and no matter her reasons, her actions and inactions were not okay and therefore not forgivable. I understand her and in some ways I have compassion for her. I do not however, forgive her, as it does not serve me.

This is what serves me, this is how I healed: I held my baby (me) in my arms and cried for the times she was hungry and left in her crib alone for hours on end. I held my child (me) in my arms and cried for the times she was terrified by the Evil One, the times she was berated, the times she was made to feel worthless. I held my child (me) in my arms and cried for her lost innocence and the murdering of her voice when she was sexually abused. I held my child in my arms and cried for the moment her ability to say no was stolen and for the moment she learned to be silent. I held my teenager (me) in my arms and wept for all of her lost moments, the carefree dances and innocent high school rites of passage. I held my young adult (me) in my arms and sobbed for all of the lost experiences; things like having her first baby with a husband who loved her, a dream wedding and college graduation. I did this for four days, locked in a depressive state in my room, in the dark. I gave myself permission to take those days and weep until no more tears would come.

I gave myself those days to be sad and to tune the world out. I gave myself those days to live through my memories and to bury them OUTSIDE of myself. I felt so robbed for so many years. I felt shame for my past and that I was somehow less than everyone else. I was silent in my relationships for fear of discovery and rejection. I gave myself four days to let go of those fears and feelings. To understand that the past can only be buried once it has been faced head-on and embraced. I am not defined by my past, I am made by my past. I am resilient and I can and adapt to anything life throws my way. I choose to take the lessons that were taught to me and turn them to my advantage. I am only defined by my present choices. I am allowed to make mistakes, and I will forgive myself when I do.

MY REAL & FINAL RETURN HOME

Home isn't a dwelling, a lesson I learned very early in life. Home is in the hearts of the people who love you wholly and unconditionally. My story, this book, brought me home to the hearts that matter to me most in the world. It brought me a closeness with my children in the most beautiful tangible way. My children read and helped me to edit my story; they received answers to questions they never asked. I found out they always wanted to know how I survived and what had happened to me, but out of love and protection for me they dared not ask. The answers gave them an understanding of me. As they gained their answers and filled me with their love and compassion I realized that the one and only thing that ever mattered to me, the one thing I wanted in this world I have. The love, respect and compassion of my children. They are my home. They are my soft place to fall and I am theirs. I am home.

RECOVERING RUNAWAYS
AKA MISSING CHILDREN

Dear Recovering Runaways:

You are not alone and unloved. You are not damaged, you are a true miracle. What life did to you does not define you. What you do with those experiences defines you. Stop running, sit a spell and love yourself. Love yourself for the incredibly strong person that you are. If someone judges you for your past they are not worthy of your present, presence, or energy. Only small minded, insecure people judge others.

Grieve your losses, don't ignore them. They are real. You were robbed. You WERE mistreated. You WERE victimized. You need to grieve the death of the child and teenager that never was. You can only move forward after you let go. Bury the pain where it belongs, OUTSIDE of yourself. Take the lessons from your experiences that will serve you well and let the rest go.

Let go of anger and hate. You don't have to forgive unless you want to. The only meaningful judge of you is you.

You deserve happiness and fulfillment as much as everyone else on the planet. You are worthy. Love yourself enough to stop running and forgive yourself when you do.

TO THE PARENTS OF THE MISSING

To the parents of missing children who care: I survived for over three years on the streets. I came out the other side, I am obviously alive and breathing. NEVER give up hope, and never give up the search.

I was on the streets before the advent of social media and Amber Alerts. Given my geographical proximity to my "home" for over a year you would think I would have been found. As close as I was to home, I did not want to be found. Runaways are afraid of consequences; that is a big part of why we stay gone. We are also very good at adapting and remaining hidden.

Sadly, all I can offer is prayer and the hope that you are reunited with your missing child. I had a great many bad experiences, but I also managed to provide a life for myself much of the time. I hope with all of my heart that you leave this book with that knowledge. I more than survived through the bad, I learned from it and am a better person because of AND in spite of it all. There is always a possibility that your child will and is doing the same. There is always hope. I am living proof.

TO THE PARENTS OF CHILDREN FOUND

We are not the same children that left. We will never be the same. Please hold no expectations. We are in fact, no longer children. We have not had structure. We have not had house rules. We have survived by luck and by following our instincts. We are angry and we are sad. We don't know where we belong. We are stuck between the knowledge of how to take care of ourselves and nowhere. If there are other children in the house you cannot treat us the same, simply because we are no longer the same.

We need your emotional protection. We need counselling. We need patience. We need you to develop rules and structure with us, not for us. You need counselling, we ran from you instead of to you. You have to own that. We need counselling together to become whole.

We need positive reinforcement. We need to hear and know what we are doing right. Let us tell you our story when we are ready. Where we have been is nowhere near as important as where we are now. Where we have been should not overshadow where we are going.

IN THE END,
HAPPINESS IS A CHOICE

Through all of this, there is one absolute that I know to be true: We are truly the masters of our own destiny. We can talk about life or live it. We can write a book or read it. Paint a painting or view it. Whatever it is, whatever you goals and dreams are... you can either take action and commit, or not. The way you live your life is a choice. Happiness is a choice, your choice.

I am not an extraordinary person in terms of being any different from anyone one else. We are all extraordinary and we can choose to live extraordinary lives. Survive or surthrive. Positive thinking is the key to happiness. I know we all fall off. We all have moments of weakness. Being aware and resetting our minds is the key to success and happiness. In my darkest days I held to the thought that better days lay ahead. Thirteen and fourteen years young, cold, hungry and alone. When I was sleeping in the sauna on those unforgiving wood slats I focused on that thought. Our mindset ultimately controls our destiny. Our mindset allows up to put thoughts into actions. I am living those better days every day. Every morning I decide what kind of day I am going to have. Every morning I write my own horoscope instead of reading it.

Write your own chapters, set your goals. Be fearless; and finally, always, always be true to yourself.

- Love Marnie

THE END?

Hardly. As I pieced together my blurred memories and struggled through the telling of my story, the chronology was at times obscured. I managed to find bits and pieces of documentation and photographs I didn't realize I had. There was a moment in my late twenties where I loathed myself so much that I destroyed many of the few photos I had. I could not bear to look at that "dirty' child. In my search for my "tangible" past I found the police reports and autopsy report that were recorded at the time of my father Lenny's death. The inconsistency in the documents combined with the lies told by my mother and brother will see the light of day in my next book, including the reports themselves. I don't know if I can get the case re-opened given that my father was cremated, but I am going to try. Justice must be done one way or the other.

FINAL THOUGHTS

When I embarked on my journey to finally write the story I have been struggling with since the age of seventeeen, I had no idea where it would lead me. The healing has been immense, the lessons countless.

I wrote this book sitting in one of my favorite places, a beautiful hotel lobby close to home. I chose to go there so as not to isolate myself - and to keep my sanity. It would have been all too easy to get stuck in the dark places that I was reliving. The space I wrote from was bright and cheerful, with live musicians playing in the background everyday.

On more than one occasion or two someone would approach me, asking what I was working on. Initially I would tell them I was writing a book. "What kind of book?" or "What's the name of the book?" Something along those lines. As soon as the person - male or female - heard the term runaway, their demeanor would immediatley change in a judgemental sort of way. There would be a coolness. I didn't just see it with my eyes, I felt it with my heart. There was a time when that judgement would have swallowed me whole. Indeed, it did have an effect on me. A thoughtful one, one so powerful that it caused me to revisit the title of my book. It also caused me to research how runaways are viewed as a whole. I also tried changing my answer when someone asked about the topic of my book just to see if their demeanour would still be one of judgement.

"It's about a missing child."

One change, a simple word... Yet it brought about a completely different reaction. Sympathy and awe. "Is it your story? What happened?" My response? The truth, no change other than from the term runaway to missing.

Here are the facts. Runaway children are forced from their homes in one way or another. No they may not initally be abducted children, but once on the streets many are prevented from coming home. The National Center for Missing & Exploited Children estimates that 1 in 6 runaways reported to them were likely sex trafficking victims. In 2013 that number was 1 in 7.

The photo of me below was taken only a few short months prior to the run in which I was taken to Haulover beach and raped throughout the night. Had my rapist wanted to keep me indefinitely, or had he wanted to sell me, he could have, and no one would have ever known. Runaways are every bit as endangered as a child who is abducted. In some ways even more so. Think about it. An abducted child has the attention (and rightfully so) of the media and search teams. Other than on media like Facebook, do you ever hear about the child who ran away?

ABOUT THE AUTHOR

Marnie Grundman is a Montreal native currently residing in Toronto, Marnie is a proud mother of 3, grandmother of 2, and truly grateful for all of the blessings life has given her.

Marnie with her children and grandchildren
Tyler, Daniella, Marnie, Tommy, Jade and James

Made in the USA
Las Vegas, NV
27 January 2022